How To WRITE THEMES AND ESSAYS

ARCO

HOW TO
WRITE

Themes
&
Essays

John McCall

Associate Professor of English
Wisconsin State University

MACMILLAN • USA

CONTENTS

PREPARING TO WRITE A THEME

TO THE STUDENT AND THE TEACHER

This book is intended for the first course in composition and can be used for any level of high school or college work where the emphasis is upon the writing of expository themes.

Much of the difficulty experienced by the beginning writer is that of organization: developing and presenting a clear and logical discussion. In fact, many teachers give a theme two grades: the one "above the line" is for grammar, spelling, punctuation, and so on; the one "below the line" is for organization (see A TYPICAL GRADE SHEET at the end of this book). The purpose of this book, then, is to help a student to improve his grade "below the line."

A note about the illustrative themes included: They are merely presented as examples of a particular form of development, not as themes of A, B, C, D, or F caliber, nor as themes of a new, imaginative, or memorable kind.

Only one of the themes is an example of literary analysis—see "An Analysis of 'A Description of a City Shower'" found in the DEFINITION-ANALYSIS section. The reason for not including more themes of this type is that literary analysis is a study in itself, beyond the scope and purpose of this book. The beginning writer has far too many problems to cope with before he attempts to deal with the complexities of literary analysis.

HOW THE STUDENT SHOULD BEGIN

"How do I go about writing a theme?" If you are asking yourself this question, this book tries to answer it as directly and as clearly as possible—without "talking down" to you or oversimplifying the process. Writing themes is not easy, for besides organizing your paper, you have many things to worry about: grammar, spelling, punctuation, capitalization, details, effective wording, and so on. What you want, therefore, is a short, factual, to-the-point discussion of how to write a theme. Such a discussion is the promise of this book. A half-hour or so spent on any one section should enable you to write a theme which fulfills the requirements of whatever form of development you may select or have been assigned.

The first thing to remember is that the basic purpose of any communication is to convey ideas, thoughts, and feelings to someone else. Writing is one very important form of communication which you will use throughout your life. All writing (as well as speaking) can roughly be classified in one of four main categories: exposition, argument, description, and narrative. But these are not mutually exclusive; they can be used in combination. (These are sometimes referred to as the forms of discourse):

Exposition: This category includes most of what we write and read: textbooks, magazine articles, newspaper editorials, etc. Its purpose is to explain something: make an idea clear; convey a fact or a related series of facts; explain a process or a method, an organization or a system; etc. It includes either a presentation of factual material or an analysis of it, or both.

Argument: The central purpose of argumentative writing is to convince, to persuade the reader to adopt a certain idea, attitude, or course of action.

Description: The aim of description is to evoke the impression produced by some aspect of a person, place, scene, or the like. The writer tries to suggest in the reader's mind a picture similar to the picture in his own mind.

Narrative: The aim of narrative is to tell a story—to give meaning to an event or a series of related events. Fiction is known as plotted narrative. Non-fiction narrative writing may deal with events which are obviously significant (such as important events in history), or the writer may develop a significance in them by his particular treatment of the facts.

In high school and college the student usually has a chance to develop his skill in all four categories. But it is highly probable that most of your papers in English composition classes will be expository—that is, exposition will be their central purpose. But since all four forms of writing can overlap, any composition you write will probably combine one or more of the methods described above. For example, your main purpose may be to explain how to do or how to build something (exposition), but you can add spice and human interest to the theme by adding a flashback (narration) which includes dialogue and action from your own experience. Examples of combinations of forms are given throughout this book in an effort to show how they may be combined to good advantage. In addition, specific examples of argumentative and descriptive themes have been included.

If your teacher has assigned a particular kind of theme, you should turn to the appropriate section in this book and read it through once to learn the broad principles. Then, follow the suggestions and the list of do's and don't's in writing your paper. Also check HOW TO BEGIN A THEME and HOW TO CONCLUDE A THEME at the end of this book. After you have completed your first draft, again go over the list to see if you have correctly followed the suggestions. Check each item. Of course, double-check your theme for every item on the PROOFREADING CHART, also at the end of the book. Once you have checked each item, then and only then should you write the final version to be turned in.

COMMON FORMS OF THEME DEVELOPMENT

In many instances, your teacher will not specify a particular kind of development. Instead, the class is told to write on a particular topic, with the development left up to the student. This assignment need not be any more difficult than if the form of development were assigned. Here are some specific suggestions about the most common forms of development.

DEDUCTIVE: Use this for any topic where you have more than one item to discuss that deals with your main idea. This common form of theme development is used in perhaps 75 percent of student themes. (See p.73ff.)

INDUCTIVE: The opposite of deductive. Use it when you want to "save for the end" the main idea of your paper, when all the things you discuss lead to a conclusion, a moral, a lesson learned, a rule, and so on. (See p.114ff.)

CLASSIC: It combines both deductive and inductive forms. Use it when you wish to repeat each of your main points three times—once in the introduction, once in the individual paragraphs, and once again in the conclusion. It is used frequently in arguments, sales talks, sermons, and the like.

CHRONOLOGICAL: An easy form of development. Use it when time plays a part from the beginning to the end of your theme—a trip, a vacation, your high school years, how to do something, and the like.

DESCRIPTIVE: Use when you know enough about a subject (or are interested enough to investigate it) to provide sufficient details to give the reader a clear picture or a dominant impression of the thing described.

HOW-TO; HOW IT IS DONE: Use the former if you are sufficiently expert on the topic. It implies that you have done it. Use the latter if you know enough about a topic to write a factual theme. It frequently means that you have to consult an authority or a printed discussion of the topic. The primary purpose of the HOW TO theme is to give directions to the reader so that he can carry out the task following your directions. The purpose of the HOW IT IS DONE theme is to explain a process that the reader is curious about but has no intention of doing.

The following forms of development are used for specific purposes. In most cases, your teacher will give you the assignment.

ANALOGY: Use when you wish to explain something complicated by comparing it with something simple, or when you wish to compare two things which are ordinarily not considered to be alike.

ARGUMENT: Use this form with caution. Remember that

"Nobody ever wins an argument" implies that your theme will also be on shaky ground, chiefly because all the facts and all the details have to be considered. If assigned to write an argumentative theme, state that you will present the facts to the best of your knowledge, and state that the reader has to make up his own mind.

BALANCED: Use when the discussion in the first half of the theme inevitably and logically leads to the second half. In other words, you have two main ideas in your theme, each of which takes up approximately half of the discussion. If you are not sure of this form of development, do not use it.

CAUSE AND EFFECT: Use when you wish to show the results (effect) of some event, idea, or action. You may develop the theme by showing how the causes led up to the effect, or you can state the effect(s) first.

CLASSIFICATION: Use when you wish to show how experts classify, or when you wish to show how you would classify items which share common features.

COMPARE AND CONTRAST: Use when you wish to show the similarities and differences between two or more things.

DEFINITION-ANALYSIS: Use when you wish to categorize, clarify, or explain confusing items, or when you wish to interpret or explain the "how" and the "why" of your personal opinion.

SUMMARY: Use only when specifically assigned by your teacher.

The other forms—FLASHBACK, IMITATIVE, and IMPLIED—are usually specifically assigned or are part of another form of development. The SPACE FILLER is included as an example of what not to do.

Remember that in beginning themes, your teacher is not so much concerned about literature as he is about literacy. What your teacher is looking for at first is a theme of perhaps three hundred words that states a thesis; that devotes two, three, or more paragraphs to developing that thesis; and that gives evidence of logical organization for proper communication of ideas.

How do we start? Let's take the most common form of development, that of the DEDUCTIVE, where you make a generalization (the thesis statement) in your opening sentences and discuss two, three, or more particulars in the following paragraphs. Let's assume that your teacher has given you an assignment to turn in a theme of two pages. Two pages may seem like a huge task, especially if you have never written that much before. How to fill two pages? Let's pretend that you own some guns: a pistol, a .22 caliber rifle, a .308 caliber rifle, a single-shot .410, and a double-barrel .12 gauge. That's five guns—five paragraphs.

Let's stop a second. So you have five guns. What can you say about them? Whatever you can say about them becomes a generalization, a thesis sentence. You can make various generalizations: "My five guns have an interesting background." Then each succeeding paragraph will discuss the "interesting background" of each gun. Or, you can say "A hunter needs at least five guns to be equipped for all shooting situations." Again, you would discuss each gun in a separate paragraph, showing how each gun can be used for a particular purpose. Or, you can write about "How to aim a gun," "How to clean a gun," or "How the price of guns has gone up." If your theme becomes too long—remember a few minutes ago we were concerned about filling two pages—just discuss two or three guns.

So, you don't own guns? Have you ever owned dogs? Two, three, or more dogs can be discussed just as well as two, three, or more guns. So can your brothers and sisters, the cars you have owned or would like to own, the hobbies you have, the teachers you have, the trips you have taken or would like to take, and so on. In short, any topic that can be broken down into two, three, four, or more parts can be a good theme topic.

To show how easy the process of writing is, let's pretend that you have not five, but three guns. The title is easy: Guns for Hunting. The thesis sentence will state what the three guns have in common. Let's say that this is your thesis: "Three guns are all that are needed to hunt within this area." (Although you will use your personal experience to support your thesis, try to avoid using the first person in the thesis.) Let's put the sentence into an opening paragraph:

"At the present time, I own three guns: a Ruger Mark I target pistol, a Remington Model 600 carbine, and a Fox double-barrel shotgun. These three guns are all that are needed to hunt within this area. Let me explain."

You don't have to write any more than three sentences. A good introductory paragraph, however, should be developed more fully, stimulating the reader's interest and suggesting the tone and the method of theme development. (Quotation marks are merely to show which of these paragraphs belongs to the theme and which belongs to this Introduction. The theme when written would not have quotation marks.) You mentioned the pistol first. So, you will make it the topic of your second paragraph. Describe it and say what kind of hunting you use it for:

"*My first gun is a Ruger Mark I target pistol.* It's a .22 caliber automatic which holds nine long rifle cartridges. The barrel is $6\frac{7}{8}$ inches, the pistol weighs 42 ounces, and the sights consist of a blade front and a click rear which is adjustable for windage and elevation. I use this gun not only for target practice, but also for shooting owls, crows, and vermin. Any small game which is legal to shoot at while sitting is good hunting. Many a Saturday I have spent in the local junk yard eliminating vermin, which are always plentiful and which afford me much practice."

The third paragraph talks about the next gun:

"*My second gun is a Remington Model 600 carbine.* It holds five .308 Winchester shells, weighs $5\frac{1}{2}$ pounds, and is a fraction over 37 inches long. It's a beautiful gun and handles as though I were born with it in my hands. This carbine is perfect for hunting deer when the terrain is rough. Deer in this area are found only in thick brush, where a short rifle with plenty of shocking power and rapid firing is needed. The proof is in the field: Using this powerful little rifle, I have brought home a deer three seasons in a row."

And the fourth paragraph tells about the third gun:

"*My third gun is a Fox double-barrel .12 gauge shotgun.* It is my pride and joy. It is chambered for $2^3/_4$ inch shells, is hammerless, has an automatic safety, and has the right barrel full choked and the left barrel modified choke. This gun is perfect for the many rabbits around my home town and is also a wonderful gun to bring down the occasional duck which flies to the small pond near my home."

Now you need a concluding paragraph. You tie it in with your opening:

"In the near future I hope to buy a few more guns. But since the only game animals I have to hunt around my home town are the ones I have mentioned, the three guns I own are all I need to have a successful day's hunt."

You have written your theme. Put the five paragraphs together and they represent a competent, logical, organized presentation of a topic. The theme has a title which tells what you are going to discuss. It has a thesis which limits the area you are going to cover and also serves as part of the introductory paragraph. It has three paragraphs, each of which describes a gun and tells what hunting the gun is used for. (Note that the first sentence of paragraphs 2, 3, and 4 is the topic sentence of the paragraph.) And it has a concluding paragraph which "wraps up" the theme and makes it unified by repeating the thesis sentence. This, of course, is a very mechanical organization, and although the theme is adequate, it is not especially exciting or stimulating. Each of the paragraphs should be developed more fully with more examples.

We have mentioned the various things you can write about—hobbies, teachers, brothers and sisters, and so on. All you have to do is pick a topic that can be divided into parts. On page 15 is a little chart that can be used to help you write your first theme.

My Three_____

(Thesis sentence in first paragraph) My three _____

_____

(Topic sentence of second paragraph) My first _____

_____

(Topic sentence of third paragraph) My second _____

_____

(Topic sentence of fourth paragraph) These are my three

_____

(Fifth paragraph concludes the theme) These are my three

_____

With the blanks filled in, add a minimum of three or four sentences which discuss the words in the blanks in each paragraph, and you have a theme.

And now, turn to the section of this book which interests you or which you have been assigned and read it through. Following the suggestions and the list of do's and don't's, read the sample themes and the analysis given for each theme. Then organize and write your theme. It's not so hard after all, is it?

BUT FIRST THE PARAGRAPH

Before you can hope to write an effective theme, you must become thoroughly familiar with the development of the expository paragraph. Since the only purpose for writing is to communicate your ideas to readers, paragraphing has been developed as an easy means of letting readers know when the writer is going to introduce a new idea. This concept originated with the early Greeks (the word derives from the Greek *para*, a pause, and *graphos*, in the writing), who inserted the paragraph symbol (¶) in uninterrupted writing to let the reader know that he could pause before a new idea was begun. Although there are different types of paragraphs—dialog, journalism, mood, rhetorical—it is the expository paragraph of idea that you will use most frequently.

Planning the expository paragraph is similar to constructing a shack. First, you must know why you want to build the shack: you cannot pour the foundation until you know what purpose the shack is to serve. Second, you must draw careful plans to assure that the shack will serve the intended purpose. It would be rather foolhardy to discover during construction that you did not leave enough room for a door. Then, once you have carefully reviewed the plans and made certain that they meet your purpose, you are finally ready to pour the foundation, which is the support for your shack. Now build on that foundation while carefully following your plans. Should you decide to make any modifications, you must first modify your plans to see if the changes conform to the purpose and overall plan. Organizing a paragraph is done in the same manner as constructing a shack. It would be just as foolhardy to begin with a topic sentence without first having a purpose—a thesis. Once you have a clear thesis statement, you are ready to outline, making certain that every sentence is well thought out and relevant to the thesis. Now you are ready to write the paragraph, carefully choosing the method best suited for developing your idea. Much as the builder puts on the finishing touches, so must you write an effective concluding sentence.

The expository paragraph develops one idea through a series of related sentences. The idea is introduced by a topic sentence, which sets forth the main idea of the paragraph; the idea is developed through a series of related sentences, which support the topic sentence in a detailed logical manner with sufficient details; and it is ended with a forceful concluding sentence. The effective paragraph must be unified and coherent, and it must hold the reader's attention. Let us look at each of these characteristics individually.

THE THESIS STATEMENT: The thesis statement is the focal point of your paragraph, your controlling idea, your objective. Before you begin outlining and writing, you must have a clear idea of what it is you are trying to prove. Much as a driver must know his destination in order to plan the best route, so must a writer know his goal to write an effective paper. Think of a friend telling you a story that rambles on until you finally say, "What's the point? Why are you telling me all of this?" The "point" is your thesis. To be effective, the thesis statement must do more than simply state the subject, for example "Cats are felines." Instead it must go further and reflect an attitude, as in "Cats are an abomination." A simple statement of fact does not need to be developed or proven, but an attitude does. Furthermore, the thesis must be very specific. "Writing in class is different" is too vague a statement, but "Writing in class limits one's ability to develop his topic fully" forces you to be specific and to concentrate on proving your point.

An effective thesis must be a declarative sentence, a *statement* of the controlling idea, and not a question. The thesis should be a simple sentence or a complex sentence, for you want to concentrate on only *one* idea, and it should be in the active voice so that it does not suggest passivity. In addition, the thesis should be a universal statement rather than a personal one. For instance, don't use "I have a great deal of difficulty developing stable relationships with the opposite sex." Instead, universalize this statement with "Some people cannot develop stable relationships with the opposite sex." This enables all readers to identify with the thesis. However, feel free to use your personal experience to support the thesis. The more forceful you can make your thesis, the more forceful will be your paragraph.

THE OUTLINE: Once you are certain that the thesis statement is an accurate indication of the point you want to make, you are ready to outline the paragraph. The thesis statement will, of course, suggest the method you will use to develop your idea: *causal analysis, instances and examples, comparison/contrast, process analysis, definition, anecdote (narrative)*, or a combination of these. The outline for the paragraph should be very informal; just jot down the key words or phrases of the arguments you will use to support your thesis. After you have "drained your brain," review each item and ask yourself if it supports your thesis *and* if it adds something. If the answer is *no*, cross it out. If you have enough items left, number them in the order in which you will discuss them—either ascending (from the least important to the most important) or descending. Generally, it will be more effective to end with the most important argument, since this is what you will leave your reader with. If, however, you have too few relevant items left, you should either try to think of more or modify your thesis so that you can develop your idea more fully.

THE TOPIC SENTENCE: Whereas the thesis statement is essentially for the writer, the topic sentence is for the reader. Although it is possible for the topic sentence and the thesis to be one and the same, the thesis will generally require rewriting as a topic sentence. Remember, the topic sentence must be vivid, stimulating, and exciting, for it must capture the reader's interest. Always remember that there is nothing that forces your reader to continue reading. Unlike a listener who remains seated throughout a speech because common courtesy demands it, your reader is free to stop reading at any point. Also, unlike the listener who can interrupt you for clarification, the reader cannot. If your meaning is not clear, he will simply stop reading. Once the reader stops, there is no way you can get him back regardless of how interesting the rest of your argument may be. In addition, the topic sentence should set the tone—for example, humorous, whimsical, reflective, or satirical—and suggest the method by which you will develop the paragraph. The topic sentence could come at the end of the paragraph or somewhere in the middle, but usually, it is the first sentence. If you are a novice writer, you will find it best to place the topic sentence first.

There are essentially three types of topic sentences you can use: the direct statement, the indirect, and the rhetorical. In the direct statement you leave no doubt as to what you plan. "Student activism has forced college administrations to reduce formal undergraduate requirements" lets your reader know that you will prove specifically *how* this reduction came about or that you will give examples of the reductions. The indirect or implied topic sentence, however, only hints at the main argument. "Recently, I had an interesting chat with a lawyer about the future of television" implies that you will focus on the legal aspects of television due to the reference to "lawyer." The third type, the rhetorical question, is a device that can be used effectively to stimulate the reader's interest. "What effect will the proposed tuition increase have on minority enrollment?" raises a question that you will proceed to answer in your paragraph.

THE WRITING OF THE PARAGRAPH—METHODS OF DEVELOPMENT: It is in the body of the paragraph where you must prove your topic sentence, your thesis. If the development is weak or incomplete, then you have failed to make your point. It is, therefore, essential that you develop your paragraph fully and logically. A two- or three-sentence paragraph is comparable to a very skimpy sandwich—very unsatisfying. Although the bottom slice of bread, like the topic sentence, supports the sandwich meats, it is the meat that makes the sandwich tasty and worth eating. So it is with the paragraph. The *tastiness* of the paragraph is, in part, determined by the method of development you will use. You can choose any one of the following to develop your paragraph: instances/examples, causal analysis, comparison/contrast, process analysis, anecdote (narrative), definition, or a combination of these with one being the dominant one.

INSTANCES AND/OR EXAMPLES:

Some topics lend themselves best to be supported by a series of instances and/or examples. (Technically, instances are actual occurrences; examples are fictitious ones. However, this distinction has become blurred over the years.) In such a paragraph, you will select those instances/examples that will most effectively substantiate your main idea, the assumption being that you have many to choose from. Be careful not to use too few, leaving your reader unconvinced, nor too many, leaving him overwhelmed. The following paragraph illustrates this method:

Good teaching can be recognized rather readily. From the moment Professor Sy Kee entered the class, we knew he would be dynamic and interesting. He walked in briskly, greeted the class in a clear, dulcet voice, and made us all feel comfortable. Professor Sally Forth also exemplifies the good teacher. Her lectures are always carefully prepared, yet she affords every student an opportunity to join in class discussions. Even when few students try to monopolize the discussion, she politely, yet firmly, invites comments from even the most reluctant. But perhaps the most outstanding example of a good teacher is Dr. Frank N. Stein, who is always ready to meet with any of his students, and even goes as far as giving us his home phone number in case we have any problems with the assignments. These, and others like them, are readily recognizable as good teachers.

COMPARISON AND/OR CONTRAST:

Most significant in this type of paragraph is that in your topic sentence you must state or imply that you will make a comparison (similarities or differences of two or more items). You cannot begin discussing Macbeth's tragic flaw and then later in the paragraph discuss Hamlet's unless you stated your intent to do so in your topic sentence. Such a paragraph will lack unity.

There are two ways to organize your comparison/contrast paragraph: the block method and the point-by-point. In the first method, after your topic sentence, state all you have to say about Macbeth, and in the second *part* of the *same* paragraph, state everything about Hamlet. (Note that the quantity of information for the two does not have to be equal.) For the point-by-point method, after your topic sentence, follow each statement about Macbeth with a comparable statement about Hamlet. This method is more effective when your statements about the two are more or less equal and when the two lend themselves to a point-by-point comparison. However, to determine which of the two methods is the more effective, try your paragraph both ways.

The analogy is also a comparison/contrast paragraph. Here, rather than dealing with items that are similar—for example, the maintenance costs of the Toyota Camry as opposed to those of the Chrysler LeBaron—you point out similarities between items that are otherwise different, e.g., the similarities between writing and painting. Your topic sentence indicates the comparison: "The painter and the writer have much in common." (The second paragraph of this chapter is an analogy paragraph.) You can use either of the above two methods for developing your paragraph.

Let's look at a comparison/contrast paragraph developed by the block method:

Children growing up today do not get a chance to develop the same kind of initiative and self-reliance as the children of the forties. When I was growing up, there were no Little Leagues to organize every activity. We pretty much had to rely on ourselves. A group of kids would meet in the street for an impromptu game of punchball. One sewer was home plate, the fire hydrants were first and third bases, and the other sewer was second base. One's skill was measured by whether one was a one-sewer, two-sewer, or three-sewer hitter. If enough kids were not available, we could always play stoop ball or stoop baseball. If no one else was around, there was kick-the-can, hop-scotch, or marbles. We did not have, nor did we need, baseball fields or uniforms or coaches. Today's youngsters have all their activities organized. In order for them to play, the parent enrolls them in an organized activity, be it Little League baseball or football. The games are scheduled, the child must be transported to the field, and the coaches direct. The child has nothing to do but show up and follow directions. If Little League is not available, then the child may be sent to judo class or gymnastics or ballet. When the activity is not organized or planned, he is often at wit's end, not knowing what to do with himself. He constantly needs someone to plan his activities. These youngsters do not have the initiative and self-reliance of the children of the forties.

This paragraph could also be organized point-by-point. Every time you made a statement about the forties' child you would make a comparable statement about today's child.

However, you would find that the content of this paragraph lends itself better to the block method.

CAUSAL ANALYSIS:

Causal analysis is a common form of logical argument wherein we try to establish a clear relationship between occurrences. In a sense, every cause will have an effect that will in itself become the cause of another effect, as in a chain reaction. In most cases, however, we find that there may be several causes producing one result. For example, your failure of a course was probably the result of many factors: insufficient time to study, excessive class cuts, lack of motivation, and failing test scores. Similarly, a single cause (event) could produce several effects. For example, your failing the course may be the cause for your having to go to summer school, your losing your scholarship, and your parents grounding you and taking away your car privileges. Logically, though, you must be certain that the causes are capable of producing the stated effect, or that the effects are a logical and consistent result of a given cause. For example, does a black cat crossing your path really cause bad luck? Depending on the content, the causal analysis paragraph can either be an effect-cause or a cause-effect paragraph. In the former, the topic sentence (as well as the thesis) will be a statement of effect (the result) and the entire paragraph will deal with the causes producing that effect. In the latter, the topic sentence will be a statement of cause with paragraph content presenting the effects of that cause. In outlining the former, be sure to state only the causes logically capable of producing the effect as stated in your thesis; in the latter, include only the effects in your outline.

CAUSE-EFFECT: *Returning to college after a hiatus of twenty years affects every aspect of one's life. For one, the fear and anticipation of the first day of classes are difficult to describe. What will all those young people think of this older person in their midst? Will I be able to follow the professor's lecture and take the appropriate notes? And then there is the question of study habits. Can I still retain information as well as I could years ago? After that first day, I had other concerns. What about my library skills? After all, many of the libraries are now computerized and offer a much wider* *array of services. How about extracurricular activities? Can I partake of them without seeming totally out of place? What about my family? How can I deal with the children's needs and those of my spouse? Will they resent my taking time from them and devoting it to my studies? What about all those routine jobs around the house that will need to be delayed? I know many of my friends will resent my no longer having the time to spend with them doing all those fun things we used to do. No doubt about it, life will never be the same again.*

EFFECT-CAUSE: *My return to college after a twenty-year hiatus was prompted by many diverse factors. First and foremost was the realization of opportunities not available without that college education. Then there was the desire to complete the formal education that I had started many years ago. Of course, a feeling of inferiority was a contributing factor, especially when I felt that I did not have the knowledge to back my arguments in those discussions with my college graduate friends. The fact that my children were going to college and would soon leave the house also gave me the necessary impetus. But strongest of all was my desire to learn all that I could, and returning to college seemed to be the only logical choice.*

PROCESS ANALYSIS:

There are two kinds of process analysis paragraphs: the how-to-do-it and the how-it-is-done. In the latter, your primary concern is to explain a process the reader has no intention of undertaking. For example, one may want to know what is involved in capping an oil well without actually wanting to do it. In this kind of a paragraph, you do not have to be too exacting in describing the process. In the how-to-do-it paragraph you must be very exacting, for here your reader plans on following your directions. Your main objective here is to make your directions clear enough so that the reader will be able to accomplish the task easily.

You should be aware of several factors in writing such a how-to-do-it paragraph. First, you must be certain that you are aware of each step in the process, making sure not to leave out any critical step along the way. This may require your doing the task consciously and deliberately before writing about it. Be certain to give your directions in the proper sequential order, and also be aware of your intended reader by customizing the directions and level of directions to him. For example, describing how to use a camera requires different directions for a reader who has never used one than for one who has some familiarity with cameras. Also, the level of language would be different for a ten-year-old than for a college graduate. In addition, since you are giving directions *to* the reader, use the second person (*you*) rather than the third person, and be certain that your directions are not choppy and mechanical. Here is a rather tongue-in-cheek process paragraph:

So you're going to be stuck watching the little terrors while the wife is visiting her folks. Don't fret. Build them a sandbox, and they'll be out of your hair for a good part of the day. First, pick up four treated 2x8x10's at the local lumber yard, some angle irons, and five bags of play sand. Next, find a level 12x12 piece of land in the backyard, preferably as far back in the yard as possible. Remove whatever little grass you might have there, and cover the area with some black plastic to prevent the weeds from growing through. Now take the 2x8's, and sand the rough edges; you don't want the little tykes getting splinters that you'll be stuck removing. Place the boards at right angles, nail them together, and reinforce the corners with the angle irons. After making sure that the four corners are secure, pour the sand into the square. Throw in some pails, shovels, and old plastic containers, and the kids. Now withdraw to the patio, sink down into your favorite lounge, open a cold one, and relax. You shouldn't be bothered for a while. Hopefully, by that time your wife will have come home.

There are several factors you should note about the above paragraph. First, the tone is rather humorous, reflecting a rather sarcastic attitude towards having to watch children. Second, the writer assumes that the reader is knowledgeable about construction. He feels that he need not clarify what 2x8x10's or angle irons are or explain how to sand boards, what kind of nails to use, or how to fasten the angle irons. Also note what the writer's diction implies about the reader.

ANECDOTE (NARRATIVE):

From the beginning of time, man has always wanted to hear a story, preferably one that has action and suspense. Early writers realized quickly that one of the most effective ways to teach was by telling a tale. Sometimes the tale was an actual event, but more often it was a fictitious account whose purpose was to teach a moral. The Bible makes effective use of parables, such as The Parable of the Prodigal Son or The Parable of the Three Talents, to make the lessons more palatable. Aesop made effective use of the fable (the characters are animals that take on human characteristics—personification), e.g., The Fox and the Grapes. Other writers have used allegory (the characters and events are symbolic), as in *Everyman*, to substantiate their themes. However, in most of these tales the moral or theme of the story had to be inferred from the evidence in the story, leaving room for different interpretations. In expository writing, though, the thesis must be stated clearly. Hence, in the anecdote paragraph the thesis (topic sentence) can be stated at the beginning or at the end, but generally it is more effective at the end.

The expository paragraph of anecdote is little more than a sustained instance or example. You choose an occurrence, true or fictitious, to substantiate your thesis. Be aware that an important aspect of the narrative is that you *show* your readers and let them experience the events, whereas in the expository paragraph you *tell* them. For example, in the expository paragraph you would simply say "Joe was very nervous." In a narrative paragraph you would describe Joe's actions, reactions, and movements so that readers would conclude that Joe was very nervous. Thus, your writing must be descriptive, vivid, and suspenseful.

Since you will be dealing with only one instance, choose the events carefully. Remember, you are not in a court of law sworn to tell the whole truth and nothing but the truth. Like a sculptor working with marble, chip away the irrelevancies, and like the sculptor working with clay, add to the basic story to enhance your anecdote. In narrative writing, you are like a god: you can create what you want. Also remember that you must stimulate your reader from the start;

hence, you may want to begin your story *in medias res*, in the middle, and then fill in the details through flashback.

As I lay in my parents' bed—a privilege extended only when I was sick—practically hidden beneath the big fluffy featherbed, the heavy and delicious aroma of roast duck and freshly baked apple strudel penetrated my clogged nostrils. Listening to my mother bustling in the kitchen baking and cooking for the Sabbath meal, I felt the promise in the misty October air of a nice winter filled with ice-skating and sleigh riding. The sudden loud banging on the door interrupted my reverie. As my mother approached the front door, she almost jumped back with fright. The tall, heavy shadows through the frosted glass told who it was before she heard the gruff "Gestapo." Two Storm Troopers, black boots glistening, black uniforms meticulously pressed with the swastika prominent on the arm, stomped in. Gruffly, they informed her that we had ten minutes to pack a few belongings before they took us away, where they would not say. "Aber, Herr Leutnant," my mother pleaded, "my little boy is sick. I cannot leave him alone." There was a flicker of compassion in the lieutenant's eye as he informed my mother that an ambulance would be sent for me, and they would be back for my parents. But they never did come back. At least one member of Hitler's elite had some element of humanity still left within him.

DEFINITION:

Aside from the full-length essay of definition, there are times when you will need to define a term or concept within a longer paper. It may be a technical term that you must define for your lay reader, or a slang expression, or an abstract term, but never a concrete one. After all, we all know what a table or a lamp is, but we do not necessarily agree on the meaning of *hate, desire,* or *intellectual ability. Democracy* has one meaning for Americans and another one for the Chinese. When your interpretation of a term differs from that of others, you will need to define it in such a way that your reader will know what it means to you.

Philosophers and poets have been trying to define for us abstract concepts for ages, and they continue to do so today.

What is the meaning of *faith*? Do we all agree on what constitutes *justice*? What about *sexual harassment*? What really is a *student*? Does *freedom* mean the same thing to you as it does to your parents? The problem rests with how to define terms most effectively.

There are several different methods that you can use. However, you must be certain in describing what the term means to you. Do not tell us what the dictionary says—we can look in the dictionary ourselves—unless you plan to use the dictionary definition as a jumping-off point to show how limited or erroneous it is. Once you have ascertained its meaning to you, you might want to define the term by citing a series of **instances and examples** that illustrate its meaning. Or you might want to **compare or contrast** it to something else. For example, you could define *love* by comparing it to *infatuation*. Or, like Robert Burns, you could compare love to "... a red, red rose/That's newly sprung in June" or to "... a melody/That's keenly played in tune." You could tell us what it is not. Shakespeare tells us that "... Love is not love/Which alters when it alteration finds,/Or bends with the remover to remove." You could use an **anecdote** that would be illustrative of your definition. You could even use process analysis to describe the steps involved in falling in love. **Causal analysis** is another means by which you can discuss the causes of love or its effects. The essential element, though, is that regardless of which method or combination of methods you use, your meaning must be crystal clear. The definition is effective only when the reader can come away from your paragraph feeling, "Now I know what he means by *love*, and I totally agree," or "... and he's off the wall," or "... and some of his observations are valid but others aren't."

Don't forget that a definition paragraph must have a topic sentence, a controlling idea. With the possible exception of the anecdotal definition, the topic sentence should be the first one. Also be sure that it includes the word being defined, usually as its subject: "Poverty is not limited to having insufficient funds."

One last point. Just as in any type of writing, the definition does not have to be serious and reflective, but instead could be humorous. It is up to you to determine the tone.

In the following definition paragraph, the writer states a simple definition of the term he will define, *euphemism*. He then develops his definition by contrasting the acceptable uses of euphemisms with those he considers offensive. The comparison/contrast paragraph is organized in the block form, and each use is supported by a series of examples culled from the euphemisms currently in use.

Euphemisms, which substitute a pleasant term for something basically unpleasant, have been in use for ages. In the best scenario, a euphemism will spare someone's feelings or avoid using words society finds offensive; in the worst, euphemisms are used to deceive. Telling a friend she is pleasingly plump is not as offensive as saying she is fat. Reporting that someone passed away instead of dropped dead softens the blow. Referring to children with learning difficulties as exceptional children avoids stigmatizing them. Asking for directions to the rest room is less offensive to many than asking for the toilet. Even referring to bathroom plungers as hydroforce blast cups, gas station attendants as petroleum transfer engineers, and garbage collectors as sanitation engineers could be construed as an attempt at humor or kindness. However, euphemisms are being used more and more to deceive. When tax increases are called revenue enhancement and killing people is referred to as "unlawful or arbitrary deprivation of life," deception is the intent. Calling short people vertically challenged and the potential firing of employees as being "selected out," or "nonrenewed," or "excessed," or, worse, "career alternative enhancement programs" is misleading—and cruel. Even referring to a junk yard as an "auto parts reclamation depot" or a used car as "previously driven" has no purpose other than to mislead. When euphemisms are used to avoid bluntness and hurting people, they are commendable; when used to deceive and corrupt, like calling apartheid "cultural group concepts," they present a distinct danger to society.

PARAGRAPH UNITY: Perhaps the most critical aspect of paragraph development is unity, the development of one idea. You must be certain that every sentence relates to the topic sentence (the thesis) and develops the idea stated therein. Think of your paragraph as a freight train, with the locomotive as the topic sentence pulling the train and determining its destination. The trainmaster must be certain that every car in the train—each sentence—is headed for the same destination as the locomotive; you can't have a car with merchandise for Miami if the train is scheduled for Los Angeles. The caboose becomes your concluding sentence.

There are several ways in which you can ruin the unity of your paragraph. The most common way is by including some irrelevant statement, something you thought of while writing. This you can avoid by carefully outlining and then following the outline slavishly. Another is by changing your viewpoint. If, for example, your goal is to balance the pros and cons of changing the legal drinking age to eighteen, you cannot conclude by favoring one over the other. Changing your tone will also affect the paragraph unity. If your tone is reflective, you cannot suddenly become sarcastic. Choose one tone and stick to it throughout your paper.

Some of the sentences in the following paragraph are irrelevant. See if you can identify them.

(1)*There has been a long history of racial prejudice in America.* (2)*It all started with the arrival of the Pilgrims, who looked upon the natives as an inferior, heathenistic breed.* (3)*It was given a major impetus in the seventeenth century with the importation of Negro slaves to work the plantations.* (4)*Their white masters considered them property to do with as they wished, a view reinforced by the Dred Scott decision.* (5)*Fortunately, there were those who saw the injustice in this, and the conflict between them and the slave owners eventually led to the Civil War.* (6)*In 1863 Lincoln signed the Emancipation Proclamation, freeing the slaves.* (7)*After a short period of seeming equality during the Reconstruction Era, the Negro found himself once again being treated as an inferior.* (8)*The Ku Klux Klan and the segregation laws of the South enforced racial prejudice.* (9)*Negroes had to sit in the back of the bus, use separate water fountains and toilets, and attend separate schools.* (10)*It was not until the civil rights movement of the 1950s and 60s that official discrimination began to disappear.* (11)*But there is still a long way to go before racial discrimination is ended in this country.*

The unity of the paragraph is weakened beginning with sentence 5. The writer begins to go off on a tangent from his stated thesis: the history of racial prejudice in America. Although the thought is relevant to the preceding sentence, it does not develop the topic sentence. The same holds true for sentences 6 and 7. The next three sentences are back on target, but the concluding sentence changes the viewpoint from objective to subjective, weakening the unity once again.

PARAGRAPH COHERENCE:

Coherence is what determines whether your paragraph makes sense. You must make sure that your sentences are presented in a logical sequence so that your reader can readily follow the development of your thesis. Again, if you think of that freight train, it is the couplings that hold the cars together, insuring that all the cars will arrive at the same destination as the locomotive. In the same way, you must supply the link between the sentences. Remember, your reader has no idea what is on your mind, so you must give him the proper directional signal to indicate what is to come and how it relates to that which preceded.

There are several ways of achieving coherence. One way is through organization. Arrange your sentences in chronological order or order of importance, either ascending or descending, or use space order. Another method is the use of transitional words or phrases, such as *however*, *moreover*, *nevertheless*, *on the contrary*, *similarly*, *therefore*, *first*, and *for example*. You can also repeat the key word or use a synonym. Pronouns are effective as well, since they refer the reader to the antecedent. Other methods are the partial restatement of ideas, use of parallel grammatical structure, and consistent use of the same point of view. You may use these methods in combination. Be aware, however, that you can have transition without having coherence. "Brunhilde drinks beer. She is, however, one of the great beauties of our time" makes no sense. Although "she" and "however" connect the sentence to the preceding one, there is no logical relationship between the two. Ask yourself whether every sentence in the paragraph logically follows the preceding one. If the answer is yes for all of your sentences, your paragraph should be coherent.

ADEQUATE LENGTH:

Unfortunately, there is no magical number of words or sentences that will determine whether or not your paragraph has been developed adequately. It is safe to say, however, that although a paragraph must have a minimum of three sentences, one that short will generally be too skimpy. You must be sure that you developed your idea fully enough to convince your reader. Perhaps a good rule of thumb is to make sure that your paragraph is long enough to cover the subject, yet short enough to be interesting.

TITLES:

Yes, your paragraph, like everything else you write, must have a title. It is the title that will determine whether someone will choose to read your selection. Think of how you choose the articles to read in a magazine: it is the title that attracts or repels you.

Your title can be either a direct statement of your main idea or an implied one. When Ralph Waldo Emerson wanted to express his views about self-reliance, he simply titled the essay "Self-Reliance" since he was directing his thoughts to those readers interested in the subject. However, if you want to reach a broader audience, you may have to trick them into reading, as Heywood Broun did by calling his essay on self-reliance "The Fifty-first Dragon." You can also make effective use of allusion, whether literary, biblical, historical, or mythological, wherein you hint at your topic. Hemingway's *For Whom the Bell Tolls* lets the reader familiar with John Donne's works know immediately what the theme of the book will be.

To be effective, your title must accomplish several things. Primarily, it must capture the reader's interest, whetting his desire to read your selection. Next, it must give a clue to the thesis: use your thesis as the basis for your title. It should also reflect your tone. Don't use a humorous title if your treatment of the topic is serious. But, above all, it should be short and pithy. It is strongly recommended that while outlining you jot down a working title that you can then polish and refine for your final draft. Don't leave it for an afterthought; the title is much too important for that.

If you follow the advice given in this chapter, you should be able to write a unified, coherent paragraph. Unfortunately, this is no guarantee that it will be a stimulating, dynamic piece of writing. Style, sentence structure, grammatical correctness, diction, spelling, and punctuation are all contributing factors. But learning to write a correct paragraph is a good beginning.

Now that you have mastered the art of writing the expository paragraph, you are ready to tackle the theme. Just remember that the principles of effective paragraph writing are very similar to those for theme writing. The theme is nothing more than an expansion of paragraph organization.

FORMS AND METHODS OF DEVELOPING THEMES

Now that you have become more adept at writing the expository paragraph, you are ready to tackle the longer paper that is called a composition, an essay, or a theme. Although the terms are somewhat interchangeable, there are some slight differences among them. A *composition* technically is any piece of writing that one "composes" as opposed to something simply copied from another source. A *theme* is strongly indicative of the primary focus of the piece: a single major controlling idea. The *essay*, from the French *essai*, meaning to try or attempt, is an expression of the writer's opinion on any topic. In essence, an expository piece of writing is basically all three, although *theme* is probably the most accurate term and the one that will be used here.

The theme is little more than the paragraph—the one idea—more fully developed. Your topic sentence becomes the basis of your introductory paragraph, the developmental sentences become the bases of your body paragraphs, and the concluding sentence becomes the basis of your concluding paragraph. In the introduction you tell the reader what you plan to do; in the body you do what you said you were going to do; and in the conclusion you tell him that you have done it. The methods of development are the same as for the paragraph, e.g., comparison, causal analysis. Again, you must be certain that your entire theme is unified and coherent, and that you have a dynamic title that will get your reader interested. Simple, isn't it?

ANALOGY

An analogy is defined as a relation or resemblance existing between two things that are basically different; that is, one thing is like another thing in that they have similar characteristics, features, or effects. The more the two things share similar attributes the more they are like each other. Of course, the two things are also different in other respects. One is more advanced than the other, or it is more complicated than the other, or it is composed of the features of the other but also has additional features. In short, two things are discussed in terms of each other either to show how much they are alike or to explain how the "complicated" is really the "simple" with advancements.

Thus, we can have analogies made between things at or on the same level: a photograph and a painting, a piano and an organ, rugby and football, a chicken and a pheasant, a truck and a tractor, or stew and soup. Or, we can make an analogy between things on different levels: a child's balloon and a jet engine, a scout and a soldier, checkers and chess, a kite and a glider, or building a doghouse and building a home.

APPLICATION: Now study the suggestions and read the list of do's and don't's. Then read the theme, including the analysis given. As you read the theme, refer to the suggestions and the list to see how the theme has implemented them. Once you have a good idea of what to do, look at the suggested list of topics and decide what your topic will be. When you have written your first draft, recheck the suggestions to see if you have included everything.

SUGGESTIONS: The analogy is developed using one of the standard forms, usually DEDUCTIVE, INDUCTIVE, COMPARE AND CONTRAST, etc. Most themes based upon analogy are relatively short, chiefly because sustained analogy is either impossible, too strained, or because it becomes an exercise in trying to find similarities.

In a sustained analogy, you can either point out similarities in one paragraph, dissimilarities in another paragraph; or you can do both in one paragraph. (See both forms of COMPARE AND CONTRAST.) There is no formulaic conclusion in an analogy. (See HOW TO CONCLUDE A THEME.) As stated in the first paragraph above, most analogies are but part of another form of development.

DO'S AND DON'T'S:

1. Most analogies imply that the common, the simple, the known is used to explain the uncommon, the complex, the unknown. Or, to put it another way, analogy is used when the complex is explained by breaking it down into simple parts with which the reader is familiar.

2. Make sure that the known is known to your reader. Generations of students have smiled at Samuel Johnson's definition of "network"—"anything reticulated or decussated"—as being more complex than the thing defined.

3. Be sure also to say why the complex is not like the simple. For example, a theme describing college to a group of high school students would point out both similarities and dissimilarities. See COMPARE AND CONTRAST.

4. Most of our everyday inferences are by analogy—from past experiences to future predictions. Most analogies are brief. Most analogies are found in other forms of writing: DEDUCTIVE, INDUCTIVE, COMPARE AND CONTRAST.

5. Literary analogies are called similes or metaphors and are used in describing, explaining, arguing, and the like.

6. Don't use figures of speech and let it go at that. Thus, to say that A is like B is not enough. You must explain why A is like B, what they have in common and how they differ.

7. Don't use false analogy. That is, make sure the things in the analogy are similar, that the simple is a logical simplification of the complex or a logical simplification of part of the complex. If things are alike in one way, they may not be alike in others.

8. Don't try to explain the very difficult unless you are familiar with it.

9. Remember that no analogy is exact. The complex is only partially explained by the simple.

10. Check the PROOFREADING CHART.

SAMPLE THEME—ANALOGY—ITEMS ON DIFFERENT LEVELS:

The Queen Bee

After I pledged a fraternity, I became aware of a type of girl on campus who is highly analogous to the queen bee in a hive. I think that the resemblance is remarkable.

The queen bee in a hive represents true royalty. Her instincts tell her that there can be only one leader in each hive. For this reason, she is quick to destroy or drive away any opposition. All the other bees live to serve her and to keep her well fed and protected. The male bee is of no value except as a mate for the queen. He serves no other purpose, such as producing honey or fighting enemies of the hive, as do the workers and the guard bees. Were it not for the queen, these drones would be killed or banished. The workers supply the queen with honey. The guards protect her with a barbed weapon called a stinger. In short, it appears as though thousands of bees exist solely to serve the queen bee.

Similarly, many sororities have a queen bee, a girl who represents true royalty. Any slight threat of opposition which might come from the "workers" or the "guards" meets with sudden and sure retaliation. Accordingly, they seldom show any signs of opposing her. Even a brief acquaintance with a sorority leads one to believe that all the other girls in the sorority exist to serve their "queen bee." She gets first choice of the males on campus who are leaders, wealthy athletes, or who have positions of power. These males become her escorts, her dates. Any other male not fitting into the above groups is automatically a "drone," and he is left for the inferior bees to fight over. The workers and the guard bees in the sorority serve the same functions as their counterparts in the hive. They maintain their queen's room, her clothing, her reputation—and frequently her scholastic standing. They are at her beck and call to serve as needed. On the whole, the girls seem to regard their queen with the same respect and awe that the bees regard their queen. Rather than a stinger, however, the girls have an equally pointed and deadly weapon—their tongues. A tongue, as any male knows, can paralyze or destroy an enemy as surely as a bee's stinger.

And so, the next time you are walking past a sorority house and hear a buzzing within, do not think that your ears are playing tricks. You, my friend, have just come across a real, honest-to-goodness, grown-up hive of human bees.

ANALYSIS: This theme also begins with a short paragraph which effectively presents the author's topic. The second sentence promises the reader a "remarkable" resemblance, and the author does a good job in fully developing the resemblance. However, the introductory paragraph should have been developed more fully. This could have been done by giving the points to be compared in the body paragraphs. The closing paragraph also should have been developed more fully. Remember, a two- or three-sentence paragraph is too skimpy to really develop an idea adequately.

There is a logical development in paragraphs two and three. Obviously, the queen bee and her role in the hive must first be discussed. Then, with the effective transition "similarly," the author switches to paragraph three to point out the "remarkable" analogy presented by the sorority "queen bee."

The conclusion is short, yet effective, in that it ends with the same tone—sarcastic, perhaps, but yet in keeping with the theme.

Note that this analogy effectively discussed the complex (the sorority queen) in terms of the simple (the queen bee in the hive).

SUGGESTED TOPICS FOR ANALOGY THEMES:

1. A painting and a theme

2. Psychology and religion

3. Teachers and coaches

4. Contact lenses and eyeglasses

5. Roller skating and ice skating

6. Kissing a frog and a prince

7. Going to school and going to work

8. Love and the flu

9. Physical and mental training

10. A book and a movie

The above suggested topics, as all other such suggested topics in this book, should be limited further. Choose some aspect of a topic that you can discuss fully within the word limitation and that would be meaningful and informative for your intended reader.

ARGUMENT

Handbooks (see the Bibliography at the end of this book) usually devote many pages to themes which present an argument, because argumentative themes are very difficult to write. The difficulty does not lie in the organization of the theme. Rather, it lies in having correct logic, in presenting suitable evidence, in making a valid generalization from the evidence presented, and, of course, in presenting a better argument than one's opposition.

An argumentative theme is one which presents and develops reasons which lead to a generalization, or a conclusion, which in turn leads to an application. Thus, we present a number of instances of X causing Y to happen, and we then say that we should remove or modify X if we do not want Y to happen or if we want Y to happen in another way.

Because of the many difficulties involved, therefore, unless you have been specifically assigned to present an argument, or unless you have had special training in debating and logic, do one of two things: 1) avoid controversial topics, or

2) state you are merely presenting the two sides of an argument in order to allow the reader to decide for himself.

APPLICATION: Now study the suggestions and read the list of do's and don't's. Then read the theme, including the analysis given. As you read the theme, refer to the suggestions and the list to see how the theme has implemented them. Once you have a good idea of what to do, look at the suggested list of topics and decide what your topic will be. When you have written your first draft, recheck the suggestions to see if you have included everything.

SUGGESTIONS: Present the cause, reasons, and history of the controversy in the first paragraph. Tell the reader where you stand. Your conclusion will reaffirm your stand. If you wish to remain neutral, tell the reader that you are presenting both sides and that he is to make up his own mind.

In the second paragraph you can use one of two forms: Form 1: Discuss all of one side. It may take more than one paragraph. Form 2: Discuss point 1 of each side. If you have chosen sides, tell the reader why your side is the better one.

The following paragraph(s) is developed similarly: Form 1: Discuss all of the other side. Again, it may take more than one paragraph. Be sure you cover all the points made in the paragraph above. Form 2: Discuss point 2 of each side. If there are other sides, present them in succeeding paragraphs. If you use Form 2, use a separate paragraph for each subsequent point. As in the previous paragraphs, if you have chosen sides, say so.

In your conclusion, if you have chosen sides, reaffirm that your side is right because of the preceding evidence. If you remain neutral, tell the reader to decide.

DO'S AND DON'T'S:

1. Argumentative themes in which you take sides are extremely dangerous. Controversial subjects require much thought and research. Then, too, if you choose a harmless topic, you run the danger of writing a series of platitudes.

2. Use familiar subjects—campus politics, school activities, and the like.

3. Most argumentative themes imply that you take sides. If you write such a theme, tell the reader quickly which side you support. At the end of each paragraph, review why your side is right. In your conclusion, state that, for the reasons discussed, your side is right.

4. If you intend to remain neutral, quickly tell the reader that you are going to present both sides and let him make up his mind. See COMPARE AND CONTRAST.

5. No matter what approach you take, you must use up-to-date facts, figures, charts, quotations, authorities, and the like, for both sides. Do not use partial proof if it does not give an accurate account of your source. If you are quoting, be cautious in your use of ellipses, especially if the omitted material changes the meaning of your original source.

6. Define your terms. Be specific in what you mean by your terms.

7. Avoid generalizations by others or by yourself. Also avoid faulty logic, faulty analogies (see ANALOGY), inadequate presentation of evidence.

8. Remember that an argument must present strong evidence on all sides. If you choose a one-sided argument (for example, The Value of an Education), you are really not arguing. Such one-sided topics are best presented using other forms.

9. Avoid trying to disprove all that the opposition claims. Give credit where it is due. An argument that is willing to compromise on some issues is likely to be more fair and reasonable than one which stubbornly says that the opposition is completely wrong.

10. See also BALANCED, "The Proposed Honor System."

11. Check PROOFREADING CHART.

SAMPLE THEME—ARGUMENT:

Speak English!

Practically every week there is at least one article in the local newspaper debating whether or not bilingual education is advantageous to students. This, unfortunately, is not a recent concern. During the sixties and seventies it was fashionable in educational circles to stress the individual's right to retain the language and speech pattern of his native culture. In New York City, there were those who advocated that "Black English" should be accepted in schools as a viable alternative to standard English so that the child's pride in his culture and heritage be not destroyed. Those fostering bilingualism use similar reasoning. However, bilingual education is a disservice to the youngsters, for it weakens their ability to express themselves forcefully and accurately in English, the daily language of this country. Even writers such as Richard Rodriguez and William Raspberry, who have a strong interest in retaining the cultural values of their respective minorities, recognize the importance of children learning standard English. As Raspberry pointed out in one of his articles, "Standard English...marks a person as educated."

English is, after all, the language of the continental United States, and in order to succeed one must have a good command of standard English. It is imperative that one develop an ability to read with understanding and insight, to be able to recognize the nuances in phrasing and an author's use of diction and style. Equally as important is the ability to write clearly and coherently, to organize one's ideas, and to convey them to a reader in effective prose. But perhaps most important is to be able to speak the language, to phrase one's thoughts so that there is little room for misinterpretation and misunderstanding. All of these skills are difficult to attain, but especially so for the child who is not constantly exposed to English.

Although bilingualism has its merits, they are outweighed by its negative impact. Students who are bilingual tend to rely on their native tongue, the language spoken at home. They tend to think in that language and then translate their thoughts into English, thus often creating awkward and unidiomatic constructions. The emphasis on the native tongue also is a hindrance to accurate pronunciation. Many bilingual college students have bemoaned that they were not exposed to English in the home and that they received bilingual education. They have found themselves at a distinct disadvantage throughout their schooling and in the work force. They have found that their difficulties with English have limited their choices.

As much as we like to talk about America being a multiethnic, multicultural, multilingual society, there is no escaping the reality: the language of the country is English, and without mastery of standard English, people's opportunities and choices are limited. Their chances of deriving the full benefits from their education are restricted; their chances of getting into a good college are greatly reduced; their chances of availing themselves of all those opportunities for which a command of English is a prerequisite are nonexistent. In short, educators and parents who do not insist on children speaking English are doing them a great disservice; they are not preparing them for the future. So let us immerse students in English from day one. Let both teachers and parents stress the importance of speaking English.

ANALYSIS: In the introduction, the writer leads into his thesis by giving some historical perspective to bilingualism. He states his thesis—"However, bilingual education is a disservice to the youngsters..."—in the middle of the paragraph. He supports this stand by referring to two noted columnists with similar views.

In the body of the paper, the writer supports his thesis. In the first body paragraph he presents general arguments why a command of English is important. In the second body paragraph he becomes more specific, pointing out the difficulties faced by students who were educated and/or raised bilingually.

The concluding paragraph comes full circle to the argument presented in the introduction: mastery of English is critical for success. The writer stresses the limitations that one deficient in his command of English has. He ends his theme on a strong note to both teachers and parents to stress the importance of speaking English from the beginning.

SUGGESTED TOPICS FOR ARGUMENT THEMES:

1. Should a student "snitch" on cheaters?

2. Commuting *vs.* living at college

3. Outlawing guns

4. University *vs.* private housing

5. Fraternity life *vs.* independent life

6. Education or experience

7. Lowering the drinking age

8. Women in combat

9. Athletic scholarships

10. Scholarship *vs.* activities

BALANCED

A balanced theme is one in which the first half of the presentation logically and inevitably leads to the second half. In short, it is a theme of two parts: the facts, the details, etc., of the first half result in the effect or the conclusion which the second half discusses. Thus, while a deductive development has the generalization early in the theme, and the inductive development has the generalization late in the theme, the balanced development has its generalization, its key statement, its thesis, in the middle of the theme, and the remainder of the theme discusses it.

Be sure of one thing when using the balanced form: ask yourself if either half can stand alone. If so, your theme is incorrect. This faulty development is called "broken-backed." The one sure way to avoid it is to have your first half cause the second half: a week's rain brought on this result, the following violations brought on this rule, if that occurs then this will happen, and so on. If you are still not sure of yourself, choose some other form of development.

APPLICATION: Now study the suggestions and read the list of do's and don't's. Then read the theme, including the analysis given. As you read the theme, refer to the suggestions and the list to see how the theme has implemented them. Once you have a good idea of what to do, look at the suggested list of topics and decide what your topic will be. When you have written your first draft, recheck the suggestions to see if you have included everything.

SUGGESTIONS: If writing a "come on" theme, you will have two or three paragraphs before generalizing. If writing a "switch" theme, you will discuss all of A before discussing all of B. (See COMPARE AND CONTRAST, Form 1.) Your "come on" may well continue for another paragraph or two, depending upon the amount of detail you present before reaching your topic or thesis sentence.

The generalization or thesis is placed in mid-theme. If contrasting, use words like *but, on the other hand*. If comparing, use words like *similarly, also, in a like manner*. (See COMPARE AND CONTRAST.) After the reason for your "come on" has been stated, develop the generalization further in preparation for the conclusion. If you have "switched," you devote the remainder of your theme to whatever you switched to. The conclusion for either the "come on" or the "switch" could restate your generalization, or it could conclude by commenting on both A and B.

DO'S AND DON'T'S:

1. Unless you are sure of yourself, do not wait until mid-theme to state your thesis or generalization (the "come on" approach). It is safer to use the DEDUCTIVE approach, especially if you will do nothing but ramble until you state your thesis.

2. The balanced form using the "switch" approach is similar to COMPARE AND CONTRAST, Form 1. This balanced form implies that the two things under discussion are dependent upon one another, or are opposed, alternate choices, and the like.

3. If you are contrasting, use such words to introduce the other point as "But," "On the other hand," "If we look at the other side," and so on.

4. If you use the "switch" approach (where the topics are dependent upon each other), use such words as "Similarly," "In like manner," "Also," and so on.

5. Be careful that you do not have a "broken-back" theme. That is, if you are using the "switch" technique, be sure that the topics are mutually dependent. Do not write a theme, for instance, in which the first half talks about your home town, and the second half about your pets. The "switch" technique is best used for two sides of an argument, for comparing and contrasting, and the like.

6. For another type of balanced form, see CLASSIC.

7. Check the PROOFREADING CHART.

SAMPLE THEME—BALANCED:

The Proposed Honor System

The Student Council has been spending a great deal of time debating the merits of installing an honor system on campus. All sorts of suggestions are being made about what an honor system should be, but basically it seems to be concerned with the book store's acquiring "little blue books" which the students will use when writing examinations. On the cover of the booklet will be a statement to the effect that the student signs his name in good faith that he has not cheated on the examination. Of course, there is a place for the student's name on the booklet immediately below the pledge. The student could sign his name somewhere else on the cover if he so wishes, and the teacher could then interpret it in any way he wished.

Another possibility suggested for the honor system is that the teacher will not have to be in the room when examinations are taken. The students will thus feel that they are not being "policed." Still another suggestion is that all papers written outside of class will also have a folder which will have the pledge printed on it. Thus there will be no cheating on term papers.

On the surface, such an honor system sounds good. The school paper and the local paper will feature the installation of the honor system, and various teachers, preachers, and administrators will deliver long-winded speeches about to-day's youth being mature, honest, or what have you.

But, I have some serious objections to the honor system. My high school had the system, and for four years, I saw what really happens.

First of all, there will be cheaters no matter what pledge is signed. A student in danger of failing a course has too great a temptation placed upon him. Facing the prospect of fail-ing, of being put on probation, or of being thrown out of school, many students will grasp at any straw. I have seen it happen many times.

Second of all, I want the teacher to be in the room when I am taking an examination. I have yet to see a perfect examina-tion. Some students will always have questions about word-ing, about what is meant, about this or that or the other. Only the person who made out the examination can answer such questions.

And last of all, I do not feel as though I am being policed, nor do any of the students with whom I have talked feel as though they are cheaters because the teacher remains in the room. I understand that the school has a system whereby young faculty can expect a senior member of the department to visit the classroom for observation purposes. If the Ad-ministration feels as though its young faculty could use some on-the-spot checking, why should we students feel that we can do without it?

Thus I maintain that while the honor system sounds good, especially to the public relations department and to the do-gooders, in practice it is but a shallow system that is violated just as often as when there was no honor system at all.

ANALYSIS: We have a good balanced approach in this theme. Paragraphs one, two, and three present what the honor system will be like and how it will be regarded. Then, as illustrated in the other balanced theme in this section, we have an effective short transitional paragraph—"But, I have some serious objections ..." In a balanced theme, such a transitional technique is mandatory.

The second half of the theme is also well organized. Note the use of "First of all," "Second of all," and "Last of all" to introduce the three paragraphs. It is important that these transitional phrases be in parallel form. If you begin with "firstly," then you must continue with "secondly," "thirdly," etc. The three paragraphs also present good reasons for the author to feel as he does. The concluding paragraph is thus appropriate because it is justified by the discussion which leads to it.

SUGGESTED TOPICS FOR BALANCED THEMES:

1. Pep rallies

2. Cars as necessities or as status symbols

3. Rules for freshmen

4. College education for all?

5. Taxes for schools

6. A strong military

7. Gays in the military

8. It's a friendlier place, but...

9. Bigger and better for what?

10. Is this what we were promised?

CAUSE AND EFFECT

Cause-and-effect themes are developed using one of the other forms presented in this book, usually inductive, deductive, or balanced. In a sense, you are often arguing in a cause and effect presentation: this event or action has brought on or will bring about a certain effect (or effects). Be careful—you must thoroughly establish that the things you discuss logically and inevitably result in the effect you claim has happened or will happen.

You are familiar enough with the scientific method to know that a few experiments are not sufficient to make very solid claims. Therefore, avoid choosing controversial or broad abstract topics for cause and effect development, for instance, themes concerned with government, politics, religion, education, and the like. A short theme does not allow enough space to establish a convincing cause-and-effect analysis. Rather than try to prove something controversial to the reader which is original with yourself, choose instead to present that which others have discovered or proved, or that which happened to you—buying old cars costs you money, not organizing your studying caused you to get behind, and the like.

APPLICATION: Now study the suggestions and read the list of do's and don't's. Then read the sample theme, including the analysis given. As you read the theme, refer to the suggestions and the list to see how the theme has implemented them. Once you have a good idea of what to do, look at the suggested list of topics and decide what your topic will be. When you have written your first draft, recheck the suggestions to see if you have included everything.

SUGGESTIONS: You can begin your theme by discussing the effect (see DEDUCTIVE), or by listing the causes and saving the effect for your conclusion (see INDUCTIVE). Your following paragraphs will discuss the causes in one of several possible orders: chronological, increasing importance, causal relationship. The order depends upon your topic and your approach to it.

Begin the second paragraph with Cause 1. Use any logical order in each paragraph. You could give the effect of the cause, or you could save the effect for your conclusion. Cause 2, Cause 3, etc., can be handled in the same way, usually in separate paragraphs. Again, you could give the effect of these causes, or you could save the effect for your conclusion. Exceptions can be handled as they occur, or you could devote separate paragraphs to them.

Your conclusion can discuss your opinion, your qualifying summation, or it could show the effect the above causes lead to.

DO'S AND DON'T'S:

1. Cause and effect is essentially a "particular to general" approach (see INDUCTIVE). However, the DEDUCTIVE form (the effect is mentioned and then the causes are discussed) is frequently the form used in written reports.

2. Make sure that you have sufficient evidence. If you cannot make definitive statements, then qualify your remarks with words like *usually*, *possibly*, *it seems*, *apparently*, *probably*, and the like.

3. Do not ignore second and third causes. For instance, a successful fisherman who gets results ("effects") is successful for many causes, not just because he's using a brand name reel.

4. Beware of the fallacy of appealing to great names or to other authorities as a substitute for proving your case on its own merits.

5. Be sure that your facts, figures, authorities, etc., are valid.

6. A cause-and-effect theme is difficult to write. You will note that most discussions of the type are written by specialists. Unless you are writing about a personal experience, you will have to rely upon research to back your statements. You will frequently find topics and

authorities mentioned in such courses as history, sociology, psychology, education, and so forth.

7. Don't assume that a cause which precedes an effect is a true cause; or that two things occurring simultaneously are related. The essence of cause and effect is repeated observation—the scientific method.

8. Don't rely on generalizations. A sentence like "Everybody knows that an education is necessary" may sound good, but it is not proof. If you must generalize, use the words found in the "Qualifiers" part of DEFINITIONS.

9. Don't ignore the exceptions. That is, if the causes lead to a certain effect nine out of ten times, you must not ignore the tenth time.

10. Check the PROOFREADING CHART.

SAMPLE THEME—CAUSE AND EFFECT—INDUCTIVE:

The Bad New Days

My father grew up in the southern part of the state, and I grew up in the southern part of the state. From my father, I have inherited a love for the outdoors, particularly a love for fishing. All fishermen have a bit of exaggeration in their character, it is true, but when my father talks about what fishing used to be like in the "good old days," I am inclined to believe him. I have to take his words on trust because what we have today certainly bears no resemblance to what he describes. These are truly the "bad new days."

The Big River, Father tells me, once swarmed with smallmouth bass. The water ran clear, there were deep pools of shaded water, and any fisherman could go home with a limit. Today, inadequate laws which allow small communities to dump their raw sewage into the river have turned the Big River into an open sewer. The few fishermen who visit its banks are seeking only carp or catfish.

The local reservoir was once a two-hundred acre hotspot, or

so Father says. Today, gizzard shad and catfish have driven out all the game fish. At one time, no live bait could be used, but sometime in the past, some idiot dumped his illegal live bait into the reservoir, and inevitably the trash fish took over.

Green Lake is still a beautiful lake. It looks like a "fish" lake. It still has a reputation, largely undeserved, of being a lake for big bass. There are probably some eight- or nine-pounders in the lake. But look at its shores. Dozens of commercial and private camps, black-topped roads, rules, regulations, swimming beaches—it's like fishing in a fountain in the city square. A fisherman is hardly ever out of sight of campers, picnickers, speedboaters, and onlookers.

And Big Indian Lake can now be described as a muddy bowl. It, too, was once a fisherman's paradise. But look at it today. Black-topped roads swarming with speeders, the shores marred by beer cans and picnic litter. I imagine that a beach in a city looks pretty much like this on a Sunday afternoon. Also, sedimentation has set in. The lake is one vast shallow saucer of brown water. And when the hundreds of speedboats and water skiers finish their weekend desecrations, it takes three or four days for the water to clear.

The effect of all this is quite obvious. Fishing has become something the old-timers talk about and something the younger generation approaches in a desultory manner. Whatever may have been gained by others, the fisherman has lost out. It is a common thing for true fishermen in our section to get in their cars and drive hundreds of miles to fish. Imagine, to find fish we have to leave an area that boasts three or four lakes! And unless other areas wake up, they will eventually find that their local fishing waters have also been destroyed.

ANALYSIS: In this interesting introduction the author presents the thesis that these are "bad new days" and suggests that the facts will support his claim. Then, in paragraphs two, three, four, and five, he presents his evidence. In four well-written paragraphs, he gives the causes of the destruction of four fishing spots. Note that each of the paragraphs also has an effect. Then, in the final paragraph, the overall effect is presented: because fishing is poor, people have either quit fishing or must travel many miles to find good fishing.

The final sentence is valid: the causes and effects justify the statement. Note that this is an inductive conclusion. The last sentence could be placed at the beginning of the theme, making it a DEDUCTIVE development, or it could be used in both the introduction and the conclusion, making it a CLASSIC development.

SUGGESTED TOPICS FOR CAUSE-AND-EFFECT THEMES:

1. The causes of failure

2. Reasons for changing majors

3. A winning season

4. Our dropout problem

5. The effects of racism

6. Effects of budget cuts on education

7. Downfall of a tyrant

8. Why .... was defeated

9. Why we need more student government

10. Causes for sexual harassment

CHRONOLOGICAL

Like the DEDUCTIVE form, a chronological theme is frequently assigned by the teacher or decided upon by the student because of the ease of development: you begin at the beginning and discuss each event or detail as it actually occurs in time.

But there are dangers in a chronological development. The first is that it is frequently boring to the reader. Do not, then, try to cover each and every detail of a week's trip to New York. Rather, compress the uneventful details, major passages of time when nothing happened, and the like, into a sentence or two. This leaves you free to select the three or four high spots of the trip and discuss them in detail. Your theme will be much more interesting if you follow this suggestion.

Secondly, paragraphing sometimes is difficult. Unless your chronology can be broken down into three or four events which can serve as topic sentences, you will have to use your judgment when to paragraph.

And thirdly, select something which really is of interest to you, something that really is a high spot of your life. If you are "bored with it all," your tone will be flat, stale, uninteresting. In short, unless you are vitally enthusiastic, your theme will reflect your lack of enthusiasm.

APPLICATION: Now study the suggestions and read the list of do's and don't's. Then read the theme, including the analysis given. As you read the theme, refer to the suggestions and the list to see how the theme has implemented them. Once you have a good idea of what to do, look at the suggested list of topics and decide what your topic will be. When you have written your first draft, recheck the suggestions to see if you have included everything.

SUGGESTIONS: Your introduction could begin immediately with the sequence of events, or it could consist of prefatory remarks which tell the reader what you are about to discuss. You might also begin by using the FLASHBACK form.

Paragraphs in a chronological paper could use the usual topic sentence, or they could be built upon a period of time, or a related series of activities. Frequently a short transition can be inserted to denote the passage of time. If there is a big gap in time, you could use a short transitional paragraph.

The chronology could end in the fourth, fifth, or sixth paragraph, with the final paragraph reserved for concluding remarks. Or your chronology could end in the final paragraph, with perhaps one or two sentences serving as a conclusion. Avoid trite endings like "Tired, but happy…"

DO'S AND DON'T'S:

1. A chronological development is perhaps the easiest form of theme construction. Remember, however, that you do not have to tell everything, to account for every minute, hour, day, week, month, or year, in a chronological theme. For instance, if you are to tell about a fishing trip, the dreary list of everything that happened from the time you got up in the morning until you returned home late that evening can frequently be reduced. The rule of thumb is to begin as close to the conclusion as possible.

2. Note that using the FLASHBACK form is a frequent and acceptable variation of the strict chronological approach, especially when action is involved.

3. In HOW-TO, HOW IT IS DONE themes, strict adherence to chronology is required.

4. Especially in short papers, you can bridge the gap by using transitions. If what you did next is of little or no importance to your theme, it is acceptable to use transitions like the following: "The following day," "The next week," "Three hours later," "When we arrived," "After spending a long week," and so on.

5. Avoid saying such things as "I forgot to mention in the beginning that...," "Perhaps I should have mentioned earlier that...," and so on. Instead, go back to where you meant to say it and say it.

6. Do not reverse chronology (flashbacks are acceptable) for a paper discussing, say, your high school days.

7. Do not use an endless parade of similar expressions. Do not keep saying words like *then*, *and then*, *next*, *the next thing*, and so on. Especially avoid using the same word over and over.

8. Most chronological themes are too long, mainly because the author includes too much trivial detail. As in other forms of theme development, you should make a

preliminary plan of your approach, striving to cover only the important, interesting things.

9. Check the PROOFREADING CHART.

SAMPLE THEME—CHRONOLOGICAL:

viajo a

Journey to Nowhere

A week before Thanksgiving vacation, three of the fellows in my dormitory and I decided to go to Florida rather than go home for Thanksgiving. Accordingly, after two of them finished their eleven o'clock classes on the Wednesday before Thanksgiving, we piled into a car and headed south. Our preparations included taking beer can openers, sweat shirts with the college name on them, and a grand total of about forty dollars. We should have prepared a little more.

The car was perhaps a bit too old, eight years to be exact. It does not take a great deal of insight to predict what happened to us. We managed to get as far as Cairo, Illinois, before our first mishap, a blowout on the right rear wheel. The spare we put on didn't look much better than the tire we had to discard, but it did hold air. We wisely decided not to go over fifty-five miles an hour for the remainder of the trip, which meant that we had at least twenty-four hours of driving yet ahead of us.

From then on, we planned more carefully, or so we thought. One of the fellows from Tennessee remembered that there was a gas war going on in western Tennessee, and so we decided not to buy gas until we could save three or four cents on each gallon. As we passed through Jackson, Tennessee, we kept watching for the gas prices as we passed each service station. Again, you have guessed what happened. It took almost two hours for one of us to hitchhike to the next town, to buy a gallon of gas, and hitchhike back.

Good things and bad things, so the saying goes, happen in threes, so as we drove along farther south we kept waiting for the third bad thing. But nothing happened, at least for the next three or four hours. We planned to drive straight on through, of course, and so along about ten o'clock at night, we were sailing smoothly along somewhere in the wilds of Mississippi. I say "wilds" because when our generator finally went out, we were in absolute darkness. There was not a light in any direction, a combination of mist and fog began to shroud us, and traffic was at a minimum. As we sat there in the dark, we added to the store of curse words that enrich our language. It was around two or three o'clock in the morning before a state trooper came along—the first car to come along, by the way—and towed us into town. We slept in the car until morning. Since it was Thanksgiving, it took a great deal of persuasion to finally get a local mechanic to open his shop for us.

Our money was rapidly disappearing, we weren't even halfway to our destination, and we were far behind schedule. When the car was repaired, I got behind the wheel, made a north turn, and headed back for the campus. No one protested. We ate our Thanksgiving hamburgers at a drive-in somewhere in Kentucky. I wonder if we would have had a better time in Daytona Beach?

ANALYSIS: In five paragraphs, the author has written an interesting theme, with the chronology taking care of itself by the very nature of the theme. The introduction sets up the details of the chronology. Note that it is an interesting opening, one which attracts the reader's attention. The concluding line of paragraph one is a good foreshadowing of the events the author is to narrate.

Each succeeding paragraph handles a major episode of the trip—a blowout, running out of gas, and the failure of the generator. The final paragraph is good. While it is not a surprise ending (the introduction gives a clue that the events will be unfortunate), it continues the tone of the theme, and it ends on a light touch.

SUGGESTED TOPICS FOR CHRONOLOGICAL THEMES:

1. A day I'll never forget

2. A case of mob action

3. Man—nature's worst enemy

4. A sportsman's paradise

5. Experience pays dividends

6. A loser becomes a winner

7. How I won the prize

8. There's more to cooking than recipes

9. I learned the hard way

10. Let's save our resources

CLASSIC

The classic form of development is usually best reserved for speeches or written accounts that are long: the repetition in such cases serves to remind the listener or reader of what you are talking or writing about. In essence, when you tell a person something three times in a short theme, you are in danger of "hitting him over the head" or of leading him to believe that you really don't have much to say but keep repeating yourself to get three hundred or so words down on paper.

This is not to say, however, that you cannot use repetition in a theme. If you feel strongly about your topic, if you wish to give the impression that you know what you are talking about and have devoted long, hard thought to it, the classic form may be just the thing to convince the reader of your sincerity and strong feeling about the matter. If you have any misgivings, however, about the form, you could use either the inductive form or the deductive form and still accomplish your purpose. If you are going to repeat yourself to have something to say for a conclusion, look at HOW TO CONCLUDE A THEME at the end of this book.

APPLICATION: Now study the suggestions and read the list of do's and don't's. Then read the theme, including the analysis given. As you read the theme, refer to the suggestions and the list to see how the theme has implemented them. Once you have a good idea of what to do, look at the suggested list of topics and decide what your topic will be. When you have written your first draft, recheck the suggestions to see if you have included everything.

SUGGESTIONS: In the first paragraph, tell the reader what you are going to write about. Mention the major points of each paragraph which follows. Note that this development is very often used in speeches.

Tell the reader point 1 in the second paragraph. Begin by saying, "The first point..." or some other expression to indicate the order of your argument. Avoid such statements as "My first point..." Tell the reader point 2 in the next paragraph. Use the same type of beginning as you used in the second paragraph. Each subsequent point should have a separate paragraph.

Conclude by telling the reader what you told him. Repeat your main points, either exactly or in paraphrase. Use words like "therefore," "because of," etc., for emphasis.

DO'S AND DON'T'S:

1. Remember that to tell the reader something three times in a short paper makes for a rather tedious theme. The classic form is best used in speeches, long papers, term papers, involved presentations which are filled with many facts, figures, quotations, and the like. In long papers, in other words, your repetition is not so obvious.

2. If you must use the classic form in short themes, reserve it for arguments, sales talks, etc., where you want to stress sincerity, strong emotion, fixed conviction, and so on.

3. If you "tell me three times," rephrase your second and third telling; that is, say what you have said in your first paragraph in a different way. Again, remember how offensive television commercials are because of monotonous repetition.

4. Don't use the classic form for light, gay, inconsequential writing. Its very nature is one of firmness, sincerity, strong emotion, fixed conviction.

5. Using the classic form in short themes frequently gives evidence that a student's thinking is limited, that he is repeating himself to fulfill his quota of words. Teachers receiving this type of paper also frequently note faint pencil markings where the student has desperately counted his words.

6. The classic form is but an extension of DEDUCTIVE development. Most deductive themes tell the reader twice, but a theme which tells the reader each point only once is also quite common. See also INDUCTIVE.

7. Check the PROOFREADING CHART.

SAMPLE THEME—CLASSIC:

It's Outrageous!

As the recent flurry of activity by the Clinton Administration seems to verify, medical costs in the United States have skyrocketed in recent years, making it difficult if not impossible for the uninsured to get adequate treatment. Doctors, from general practitioners to specialists, charge exorbitant fees for office visits and for tests. Hospitals and labs often try to outdo the doctors by charging ridiculously high fees for services and medication. And, of course, the health insurance companies keep raising their premiums in an attempt to stem the flow of red ink from the cost of medical treatment rendered to their clients. Unless something is done soon to stem these runaway costs, only the very wealthy will be able to afford medical treatment.

The spiral of costs begins with the doctor. The five-dollar office visit of yesteryear has been replaced with the seventy-five-dollar fee. Some doctors will even charge an additional fee if the patient chooses to ask the doctor some questions. This is billed as a "consultation." Additional costs are incurred by mandating tests—many unnecessary but scheduled so that the doctor is "covered" in case of malpractice suits— that can run into the thousands of dollars. Recently, a patient complained to his orthopedist about pain in his heel and casually mentioned that he had an ache in his big toe. The doctor had both parts x-rayed and charged $125 *for each*. A short time ago, I had a slight hemorrhage of a blood vessel in my eye requiring laser treatment to cauterize the bleeding. After charging me sixty-seven dollars for the office visit, the doctor met me in the hospital during his lunch hour and charged me an additional $950 for the ten-minute treatment. And this did not include the hospital charges for the use of their laser.

Even worse than the charges by the doctors are those of the hospitals. The use of the laser for the eye treatment was $350. A patient who needed cataract surgery was billed $3700 for a three-hour stay. He had walked into the hospital at 6 a.m. and was in his car before 9 a.m. Included were such charges as $180 for an eye pack (a piece of gauze with two adhesive strips), $120 for a blade, $103.85 for the use of a microscope, and $23.20 for cloth towels. And this fee did not include the surgeon's fee ($2800) or the anesthesiologist's ($550). Imagine the cost of major surgery such as bypass or brain surgery. The costs become astronomical.

The health insurance companies compound the problem. Partly, they are caught in a bind in that they pay based on the "going rate" in a given area. But they make little or no attempt to try to control the cost of health care. Often when the insured complains about the high cost of treatment, the insurer assures him that the charges are within the parameters set by the company. As long as the companies continue to pay these high charges—some of them high because hospitals try to recoup lost costs for the noninsured—there is no incentive for either the doctors or the hospitals to contain costs. Given that, the vicious spiral will continue: hospitals will increase their fees; the insurance companies will reimburse and then increase their premiums.

The time has come for all concerned about these outrageous charges to make their voices heard. We must let the doctor know if we feel he is overcharging; we must ask him to justify the bill. We must check with the hospital administrator before checking in as to what the charges are and we must not hesitate to request an itemized bill, questioning any seemingly exorbitant fees. Also, we cannot meekly assume that everything is all right because our health insurer pays the bills. It is our premiums that will be increased to make up the deficit. And let us not forget to write our congressmen and make our voices heard about the high cost of medical treatment. Our health and welfare may well depend upon it.

ANALYSIS: The writer states his thesis in the opening sentence and supports it in the following sentences. Each of the next three sentences is an example of the high cost of medical care: doctors' fees, hospital costs, and health insurance premiums. These sentences suggest the organization of the rest of the paper.

In the next three paragraphs, the writer supports each of these examples of the high cost of medical care. The first body paragraph develops the assertion that doctors' fees are too high. He supports this by citing some examples of exorbitant fees. The second body paragraph, introduced by the transitional phrase "Even worse than the charges by the doctors...," discusses hospital costs, again supported by specific examples. The final body paragraph develops the third statement from the introduction: insurance costs.

In the concluding paragraph, the writer stresses what the readers must do to try to remedy the situation, again referring to the doctors, the hospitals, and the insurance companies. Note that the topic sentence, "...these outrageous charges," alludes to the title.

This theme is classic in that the introduction is essentially the theme in miniature. In theory, if not in practice, the topic sentences of all the paragraphs put together equal the introduction.

SUGGESTED TOPICS FOR CLASSIC THEMES:

1. The necessity for college

2. Our declining moral standards

3. The forgotten student

4. Do we need subsidized athletes?

5. Let's get behind our team

6. The student's right to choose his teachers

7. Equal pay for equal work

8. TV rating systems must go

9. Discrimination must end

10. Why car insurance is necessary

CLASSIFICATION

A classification theme is not difficult to write. The development you choose will probably be DEDUCTIVE. In the first paragraph, tell the reader how you would classify something—students, teachers, girls, boys, etc.—or how something is classified by textbooks, authorities, or others: roofing materials, animals, major crimes, reading material, woods. The former is your own classification and can be written without research. The latter requires the use of printed authorities; usually textbooks or trade manuals, government publications, or similar materials.

If you are writing your personal classification, be careful not to choose too broad a subject. Don't, for instance, try to classify "students." Instead, classify "Three kinds of students who share my dormitory room." Choose "Three dogs I have owned" over "Dogs." Choose "My Clothing" over "Clothing." In short, limit your classification.

If you choose a traditional classification, do not plagiarize. That is, you are permitted to use a textbook classification, but not the author's words or sentences unless you use quotations.

The question to ask is this: Does this theme sound like me or like a textbook?

APPLICATION: Now study the suggestions and read the list of do's and don't's. Then read the theme, including the analysis given. As you read the theme, refer to the suggestions and the list to see how the theme has implemented them. Once you have a good idea of what to do, look at the suggested list of topics and decide what your topic will be. When you have written your first draft, recheck the suggestions to see if you have included everything.

SUGGESTIONS: The development of a classification theme is often deductive. State your generalization in an introductory paragraph—how you or others classify your topic—and then discuss each category in separate paragraphs.

Use a separate paragraph for each division of your classification. Use any logical approach—chronological, increasing or decreasing importance, causal relationship, and so on—that best fits your topic. Be sure to continue with the type of development that your introduction and the paragraphs above have begun.

Most factual classifications (as found in textbooks) end quickly. That is, once the classification is over, stop. An original classification needs a conclusion.

DO'S AND DON'T'S:

1. Narrow your topic. For instance, rather than write about "College Teachers," limit your paper to three or four kinds of teachers.

2. If you are to write about only two classes, choose the COMPARE AND CONTRAST method.

3. Decide whether you want to write a factual classification (one that authorities have already agreed upon) or a personal classification (original plan with you). See the list of suggested topics.

4. If it is a personal classification, use a logical division. Also, do not attempt complete coverage. Use QUALIFIERS (see DEFINITIONS).

5. Do not overlap classifications. That is, make sure that a thing belonging to one class does not also belong to another class. For instance, if you classify automobiles as Imported, Expensive, and Economical, you will find that some automobiles belong to more than one class.

6. Do not over-generalize. That is, do not try to force everything into three or four categories. All students, for example, cannot be forced into three or four categories. Again, see QUALIFIERS and DEFINITIONS.

7. Your knowledge of outline procedure will be of value in determining which points are major and which are minor. Thus, each paragraph will deal with a major classification (the topic sentence), but it will also discuss minor divisions of the classification. Also, if your classification involves a number of categories, a preliminary outline will save you much time in writing your paper.

8. Check the PROOFREADING CHART.

SAMPLE THEME—TRADITIONAL CLASSIFICATION:

How Weaves Are Classified

Woven fabrics are made by the interlacing of two or more sets of yarn at right angles to produce a fabric. The lengthwise yarn is called the warp, and the crosswise yarn is called the filling (woof). The three basic weaves are called plain, twill, and satin. Many interesting effects can be created by variations in these basic weaves.

The plain weave is the simplest and most inexpensive to manufacture. The filling and warp yarns interlace alternately, forming a plain weave which is durable and used often because it is suitable for most fibers. Sheeting and wooling broadcloth are two examples of plain-weave fabric.

There are variations in the plain weave which make fabric more attractive. A ribbed or corded effect may be obtained by using filling yarns that are heavier than the warp yarns, or vice versa. The decorative blanket weave commonly used in oxford shirting is another variation of the plain weave. Here, one or more filling yarns is passed alternately over and under two or more warp yarns.

The twill weave is characterized by diagonal ridges formed by yarns which are exposed on the surface. Twill weaves are more closely woven, heavier, and sturdier than plain weaves. Gabardine, denim, and cotton twill are examples of twill-weave fabric. Variations of the twill weave may be used to form herringbone or diamond patterns in the fabric.

The satin weave is really a broken twill, but the interlacings of the warp and filling yarns are spaced to avoid the formation of a wale or twill. The satin weave produces smooth, lustrous, rich looking fabric that gives reasonably good service. Fabrics of the satin weave are more appropriate for dress or formal wear because they are not so durable as fabrics of plain and twill weaves. Variations of the satin weave may be used to make a softer, less lustrous fabric. Examples of fabrics made in the satin weave are antique satin, bridal satin, and dress satin.

ANALYSIS: This is a good theme based upon a traditional classification. Note that such a classification means that it is already agreed upon by everyone. Thus, the author's task is largely one of taking the classification and presenting it in his own words and in logical order.

Paragraphing is not difficult in a traditional classification. Here, the author chose a topic which had three or four divisions and gave enough details to explain why the divisions were made.

Note also that the tone is strictly one of giving simple, clear, direct information. There is no need in such a discussion to entertain, to strive for eye-catching wording, or the like. The presentation of facts in a straightforward manner is the dominant intention.

SUGGESTED TOPICS FOR CLASSIFICATION THEMES:

1. Careers my major can lead to

2. Divisions in my major department

3. TV programs

4. Figures of speech

5. Marriage ceremonies

6. Dormitory types

7. Show dogs

8. Musical instruments

9. Clothing styles

10. Hair styles

COMPARE AND CONTRAST

A compare-and-contrast theme implies that you will present two things to the reader—two cars, two teachers, two vacation spots—and that you will discuss their good and bad points in relation to each other. The essence of such a presentation is that you or the reader will look at all the facts or issues involved and then make a choice about which is better.

In most cases, avoid an argumentative approach with equal items—two guns, for instance. That is, do not try to prove that one gun is better than another when both are popular makes, cost and perform the same, etc. You can compare and contrast the two, but unless your facts warrant otherwise, remain fair. In short, you may choose one over the other, but do not try to destroy the one you have not chosen. If you intend to prove that X is far better than Y, turn to the argument section and follow the directions given.

Remember also that choices fall into two categories: those made on the basis of logical thinking and those which are the result of whimsy or "flipping the coin"—choices, for example, about favorite foods, clothes, guns, etc. You can, then, where appropriate, "flip a coin" in your theme and prefer one thing over another on that basis.

APPLICATION: Now study the suggestions and read the list of do's and don't's. Then read each theme, including the analysis given. As you read each theme, refer to the suggestions and the list to see how the theme has implemented them.

Once you have a good idea of what to do, look at the suggested list of topics and decide what your topic will be. When you have written your first draft, recheck the suggestions to see if you have included everything.

SUGGESTIONS: Compare-and-contrast themes usually take one of two forms (I refer to them as Form 1 and Form 2). The development of either form is essentially DEDUCTIVE or INDUCTIVE; Form 1 is more common.

Form 1: Discuss all of one thing. You could use one paragraph for all the good, and one for all the bad. Then discuss all aspects of the second item. Follow the paragraphing of the first item. If you are discussing more than two major points, see DEFINITION form.

Form 2: Discuss point 1 of A and B. Point out both similarities and differences. Then discuss point 2 of A and B. Each succeeding paragraph will discuss another point of A and B. If there are many points, use Form 1.

In your conclusion for either form, you may or may not decide in favor of one. If you intend to say that A is better than B, see also ARGUMENT development.

DO'S AND DON'T'S:

1. Form 1 is called opposing pattern; Form 2, alternating.

2. In a short paper, restrict the comparison and contrast. That is, tell the reader that you are going to compare and contrast two things, not everything. If you are going to compare and contrast three or more things, see the DEFINITION-ANALYSIS form.

3. Things compared and contrasted must be logically related. They must be alike and, of course, different. Weighing the evidence and choosing among alternatives are both involved.

4. Handle both sides in the same manner. The essence of comparing and contrasting is fairness.

5. Mere order is not sufficient. You must impart your familiarity with and interest in the alternatives you are discussing.

6. If there will be many points to be compared and contrasted (for instance, country *vs.* city life), it is better to use Form 1. It is tedious to both writer and reader to be constantly switching back and forth (the alternating pattern).

7. Do not attempt too big a topic. If you do, you will be forced into a series of platitudes or generalities which will give you organization without interest.

8. Remember that since you are comparing two things, you will use the comparative degree of adjectives. One thing will be bigger, smaller, taller, costlier, better, more nearly perfect, more nearly round, etc., than another. The superlative degree (biggest, smallest, tallest, costliest, best, etc.) is used when comparing three or more things.

9. Check the PROOFREADING CHART.

SAMPLE THEME—COMPARE AND CONTRAST (FORM 1):

Character Foil

Shakespeare makes very effective use of character foil—two characters reacting to similar situations—in *Hamlet* to emphasize Hamlet's tragic flaw, his procrastination. Both Hamlet and Laertes are confronted with the identical problem, a father both believe to be most foully murdered. Whereas Laertes, upon hearing of Polonius' death, comes rushing back to Denmark bent on revenge, Hamlet keeps delaying and rationalizing his lack of action. Through Laertes' rash behavior we can see more clearly Hamlet's inaction.

From the very moment that Hamlet learns about his father's murder, he plans to delay the need for immediate revenge. He indicates that he will "put an antic disposition on" and regrets that he was born to set things right. He questions whether the ghost was truly that of his father or some evil spirit sent to tempt him. Even after Claudius' reaction to the play within the play verifies his guilt, Hamlet still does not act. When he sees Claudius at prayer, he decides not to kill him, for that might save Claudius from going to Hell. Even when the king has Hamlet sent to England, Hamlet meekly goes along. Only through a chance attack by pirates does he manage to escape and return to Denmark, but he still does not seek revenge. After seeing Fortinbras march resolutely to Poland, Hamlet vows that "from this time forth,/My thoughts be bloody...," but still he procrastinates. When he finally does act, it is because he is forced into it. In the duel with Laertes, he discovers that he has been poisoned through the connivance of Laertes and Claudius, that his mother is dead from drinking the poisoned wine intended for him, and that Laertes is dying after having been wounded with the poisoned rapier. It is at this point with his own death imminent and the bodies of Laertes and Gertrude strewn about him that he finally stabs Claudius. One can almost assume were it not for these events, Hamlet would have continued to delay the inevitable.

Laertes, however, has no inclination to delay seeking vengeance. When he gets word that his father has been killed, he rushes back to Denmark at the head of a band of rioters to seek vengeance against the king whom he supposes to be guilty. Unlike Hamlet, he "dares damnation," for he will "...be revenged/Most thoroughly for...[his] father." He is easily persuaded that Hamlet is to blame and willingly conspires with Claudius to kill Hamlet during the duel. He is even willing "To cut his throat i' the church." Nothing will stand in his way: he must do it and do it quickly.

Through Laertes' actions, Hamlet's procrastination becomes even more pronounced. We see Hamlet questioning, delaying, and soliloquizing about his inaction. He is too much the philosopher, the thinker, the analyst. Laertes, on the other hand, is brash and rash. He does not question and he does not think. He does not worry about damnation or what will happen to the soul of his father's murderer. He and Hamlet are on opposite ends. Using Laertes as Hamlet's character foil has forced the reader to look more closely at Hamlet's tragic flaw, his procrastination.

ANALYSIS: The writer introduces his comparison/contrast in the opening paragraph by stating that he will discuss the reactions of Hamlet and Laertes to their fathers' murders. The thesis that using a character foil helps to strengthen the traits of the main character is clearly stated. Note that it is imperative, as with the topic sentence of a comparison/contrast paragraph, that the introduction be developed by comparison and/or contrast.

The writer uses the block method to develop the thesis. The first body paragraph focuses on Hamlet's procrastination, which is supported by specific examples from the play and reinforced with a sprinkling of quotations. In the second paragraph, he does the same to show Laertes' rash behavior.

The concluding paragraph again ties the two together. Here the writer points out how Laertes' actions were a counterpoint to those of Hamlet. Like the concluding sentence in the comparison/contrast paragraph, this paragraph must tie together the two items being compared.

SAMPLE THEME—COMPARE AND CONTRAST (FORM 2):

Open-faced or Closed-faced?

My title may be momentarily misleading, but it is accurate. What it means is that I have a problem deciding which fishing reel to buy, an open-faced or a closed-faced model. Terminology changes, even in fishing, and a few years ago the open-faced reel was called a "spinning" reel and the closed-faced reel was called a "spin-cast" reel. However, there was and is so much confusion about the names that many manufacturers now settle on "open" and "closed." The open-faced reel hangs below the rod; the closed-faced reel sits on top of the rod. Also, the open-faced reel has the line visible; the closed-faced has a cover over the line.

Both reels are good. Both of them use monofilament line, which has low visibility and is inexpensive. Both reels practically eliminate backlash, or "bird's-nest"—meaning a tangled line which was the curse of the older casting reels. And both reels are in the same price range so that, dollar for dollar, one cannot go wrong in buying either.

But there are differences. First of all, the open reel is about six to eight inches long. It hangs below the rod, catches on brush when I walk along the bank, and is rather awkward looking. The closed reel is compact, perhaps four inches high, fits snugly on the rod, and is streamlined. We fishermen are just as concerned about beauty as anyone; so the appearance has to be considered.

Changing lines is a bit easier on the open reel. All one has to do is loosen a wing nut, slide off the old spool, and put on a new spool. One does the same with the closed reel, but first one has to remove the cover by loosening the screw which holds it in place. For a fisherman in a hurry, this process takes another minute or two. Sometimes seconds are precious to a fisherman.

The open reel is a bit more awkward to fish with. It has a bail, a device which one has to flip each time he casts. In short casting over long periods of time, it becomes a nuisance. The closed reel, on the other hand, is controlled entirely by the thumb lever, a device which is handy, quick, and instinctively used.

The open reel has two other faults. Because it hangs below the rod, one has to buy a special straight rod for it. The closed reel, on the other hand, can fit on any casting rod (one with the handle slightly offset). There are special "spin-casting" rods one can buy, but any casting rod from four to seven feet can be used. And, because I am left-handed, I have to buy the left-handed model of the open reel. Naturally enough, there aren't many models to choose from. We lefties, however, use the regular model of the closed reel, and we have many dozens of models to choose from.

And so, considering all the possibilities, I have a problem. Eventually, I hope to own both types. But I can assure you that I am not worried; I have had a wonderful time looking at catalogs, trying reels, and talking to people who own both. Choosing equipment, in other words, is just as enjoyable to me as using it once I purchase it.

ANALYSIS: Like the previous theme, this theme is wisely developed along the lines of presenting the facts and leaving the decision to the reader. It is much better for a young writer to have this approach than it is for him to try to convince the reader that one thing is much better than the other.

Note that while we have many details in this theme, the author has chosen the alternating pattern. He could just as easily have chosen the contrasting pattern (discussing all the details about the open-faced first, and then all the details about the closed-faced reel).

Also note that the author had to make an outline before he wrote the theme. The main consideration was a logical, orderly development that did not omit any important considerations. When there are many details to be considered and discussed, an outline is of considerable help in organizing one's thoughts.

SUGGESTED TOPICS FOR COMPARE-AND-CONTRAST THEMES:

1. High school and college

2. My two friends

3. Two kinds of teachers

4. Automatic drive and "four on the floor"

5. Educational and commercial TV

6. Two literary characters or themes

7. Professional *vs.* amateur sports

8. Science and the Arts

9. Urban *vs.* suburban life styles

10. Foreign and American cars

DEDUCTIVE

The deductive development is the most common form used in writing expository themes because it follows basically the way we think and talk. A child says, "I don't like you because you're mean and nasty." This, in essence, is the deductive form: a generalization, "I don't like you," followed by the particulars, "because you're mean and nasty." Thus, any statement followed by reasons is a deductive statement.

In a theme of three hundred words or so, we develop each of the specific points in separate paragraphs. "Mean" and "nasty" in the child's statement would thus become the topic sentences of two separate paragraphs. You have a choice of giving all the reasons in your first paragraph and repeating each reason as you develop it in a subsequent paragraph, or just stating the generalization in your first paragraph and then discussing each reason in each of the following paragraphs. If you wish to go further and repeat the details a third time, see CLASSIC development. If you wish to save your generalization (the thesis sentence) for the end of your theme, see INDUCTIVE development. For a more detailed discussion of how to write the deductive form, read TO THE STUDENT at the front of this book.

APPLICATION: Now study the suggestions and read the list of do's and don't's. Then read the theme, including the analysis given. As you read the theme, refer to the suggestions and the list to see how the theme has implemented them. Once you have a good idea of what to do, look at the suggested list of topics and decide what your topic will be. When you have written your first draft, recheck the suggestions to see if you have included everything.

SUGGESTIONS: State the topic and the generalization in the opening paragraph. No matter what the topic, it can be broken into logical parts. Each paragraph which follows discusses each part in turn. Remember that neither your title nor your thesis sentence is part of your theme. You must, therefore, state your topic in this paragraph.

The second paragraph deals with the first part of your topic, which becomes your topic sentence of the paragraph (see DEFINITIONS). The third paragraph discusses the second part of your topic, which becomes your topic sentence of the paragraph. Each succeeding paragraph will discuss another major point of your topic. Use the same type of beginning used in the paragraphs above.

See HOW TO CONCLUDE A THEME in the appendix. It is acceptable to repeat your major points in the conclusion. See also CLASSIC form.

DO'S AND DON'T'S:

1. The deductive form is by far the most common development used in themes. Unless specifically instructed otherwise, all your themes could take this development.

2. Be sure to state your thesis (see DEFINITIONS) early, preferably in the first paragraph. The conclusion could restate the thesis. See CLASSIC form.

3. If you are writing an Argument, be sure to check the ARGUMENT section.

4. If you wish to "hold off" your topic until the conclusion, see INDUCTIVE form.

5. Remember that a new paragraph is a signal to the reader that you are going to discuss another point.

6. You can arrange your points so that the most important ones come last, or in chronological order, or in causal order, or in any logical order.

7. For varied ways to begin paragraphs, see "Transition" in the DEFINITIONS included in the appendix. Also check number 11 in the PROOFREADING CHART.

8. Go over your theme for the specific suggestions made in the PROOFREADING CHART.

SAMPLE THEME—DEDUCTIVE:

The Decline in Writing Skills

Although it seems that teachers have always bemoaned that students cannot write well, there can be no denying that in the past twenty-five years writing skills have hit an all-time low. This decline is due in part to the attitude of the '70s when students questioned the relevance of all undergraduate writing courses. Television and the telephone are also contributing factors in that they greatly reduce the need for written communication, at least in the students' minds. All in all, it is not surprising that so many people today have difficulty expressing themselves in written English.

The student protests of the '70s were a major factor in the decline in writing skills. At many schools, the faculty caved in and greatly reduced or eliminated freshman comp courses. At one college, where all undergraduates had been required to take two years of English, students were given the option of taking six credits of fine arts, humanities, or English. Most opted for fine arts since it required little effort on their part—and absolutely no writing. With so little demand, the English faculty dropped from seventy-nine to thirty within one year. Compounding the problem were some faculty members who felt that making students write correctly was stifling their creativity. Hence, they told students not to worry about sentence structure, grammar, or spelling but just to get their feelings on paper. The results were horrendous, with many unable to write properly.

The television and the telephone must also be held responsible for the rapid decline in writing skills. Television viewing increasingly takes up more and more of a person's leisure time, time that was often spent writing and reading. No longer will youngsters write in their diaries or try to express their feelings and thoughts in poetry. Instead they would much rather space out in front of the TV, remote in hand, and switch channels. Nor will they read extensively and be exposed to the workings of the language and absorb the nuances of effective communication. The telephone is even a greater culprit. Why write letters when one can punch in a number and speak to the other party? There is no need to write down one's thoughts and then wait for a response; gratification is immediate. Modern technology has even eliminated the need to jot notes to other members of the family: the memo unit on the answering machine takes care of that.

It is no wonder that writing skills have steadily declined over the past twenty-five years. Today's youths, for the most part, see little need for writing. The telephone is their direct line of communication, and the television supplies them with immediate entertainment. The student activism of the '70s has had its own perverse effect: it turned out a whole generation that was taught that correct writing is succumbing to the dictates of society. And horror of horrors, it is many of these very students who are now the teachers.

ANALYSIS: Following the deductive development, the writer states a generalization, his thesis, in the opening sentence and gives three major causes of the decline in writing skills: the television, the telephone, and student protests. In subsequent paragraphs he discusses both the television and telephone in one paragraph and the protests in another. He could, of course, have separated the television and the telephone into separate paragraphs if he wanted to develop each one more fully. The development could have been enhanced by citing more specific examples and perhaps some recent studies that would lend greater credence to the argument. The concluding paragraph again comes full circle to the thesis stated in the introduction.

SUGGESTED TOPICS FOR DEDUCTIVE THEMES:

1. Three types of students

2. How to study

3. Why I came to college

4. People I admire

5. My goals in life

6. Are college students "sheep"?

7. Student apathy

8. TV wastelands

9. The need to belong

10. Causes for the high cost of medicine

(See also the topics suggested in the HOW-TO, ARGU-MENT, and INDUCTIVE sections.)

DEFINITION-ANALYSIS

Definition and analysis are really two methods of explaining the same topic. When we define, we make something distinct, we explain it, we set it in a class by pointing out its characteristics. When we analyze, we break a thing down into its parts and show why each part fits into the whole. Thus, we can define what a dictionary is, or we can analyze the various functions of a dictionary; we can define what an internal combustion engine is, or we can analyze how the engine works. Thus, no matter what approach we may take, we can use both definition and analysis. Definition, in short, tells us what a thing is; analysis tells us why and how it is constructed.

As in the CLASSIFICATION development, we can either use our own personal definition or analysis, or we can discuss how authorities define and analyze something. Therefore, you are advised to turn to the classification section and read the introductory page. The same rules and cautions apply for a theme of definition or analysis.

APPLICATION: Now study the suggestions and read the list of do's and don't's. Then read each theme, including the analysis given. As you read each theme, refer to the suggestions and the list to see how the theme has implemented them. Once you have a good idea of what to do, look at the suggested list of topics and decide what your topic will be. When you have written your first draft, recheck the suggestions to see if you have included everything.

SUGGESTIONS: There is no set pattern for a theme which defines or analyzes. Once you have jotted down your ideas, arrange them in a logical order. You will discover that various developments, or a combination of developments, can be used. Suggested forms are DEDUCTIVE, INDUCTIVE, and COMPARE AND CONTRAST.

A simple form of development is to state in one paragraph what a thing is (its definition). Then, in the following paragraph, you could say what the thing is not. Or, if the thing under discussion can be broken down into kinds or types, you can devote a separate paragraph to each kind or type. A "wrap-up" conclusion may or may not be needed. See HOW TO CONCLUDE A THEME.

DO'S AND DON'T'S:

1. As mentioned, a theme which defines or analyzes can be developed using various methods. See ANALOGY, COMPARE AND CONTRAST, DEDUCTIVE.

2. No matter what your development, use many examples, details, and facts. The more information you include, the clearer will be your meaning.

3. Be sure to include what a thing is not. That is, point out how it differs from things with which it could be or often is confused.

4. Suggested ways to develop your theme include these: Break down the complex into the simple. Put something into its class. Show the origin, cause, history, and so on, of the thing under discussion; also show the result, effect, use, purpose, etc.

5. Make your definition or analysis broad enough to cover everything which falls into the class. If not, tell the reader what you are excluding and why you are excluding it.

6. Don't use the thing being defined or analyzed in your definition. For example, don't say that "a combat soldier is a soldier who combats."

7. Don't use terms which are as difficult or as abstract as the thing under discussion. Use simpler terms, more familiar objects, and the like, for your illustrations.

8. Avoid using "is when," "is where," "is how," when stating definitions. Follow the verb with a noun: A definition is the explanation of the meaning of a word.

9. Don't attempt too difficult a topic for a short theme. The danger is that you will not be thorough enough or will try to cover too much by using platitudes, oversimplifications, and generalities. Stick with the concrete at first, the visible; avoid writing about abstractions like beauty, truth, culture, education, justice, and the like.

10. Check the PROOFREADING CHART.

SAMPLE THEME—DEFINITION:

A Military Map

A military map, used by the Department of the Defense, is a graphic representation of the earth's surface drawn to scale. A military map shows features that we find on ordinary road maps, but it also includes other information of a specialized nature. There are three types of military maps that are used most often: the planimetric map, the topographic map, and the photomap. Let's look at each one individually.

The planimetric map is very much like the service station map. This map shows only the horizontal or flat position of the terrain. It includes man-made objects such as towns and roads, and natural features such as rivers, lakes, and streams.

The topographic map not only shows planimetric features but also shows relief or variations in the earth's surface. It has grid lines and a sheet number so that a soldier will be able to know his exact location or that of others. This type of map shows terrain features by various colors, such as black for man-made objects, blue for water, green for vegetation, brown for relief features, red for roads, and other colors for special information.

The photomap is a reproduction of a photograph or photomosaic. This map also has grid lines and a sheet number, but it is usually printed in black and white. Colored maps, of course, can also be used.

Military maps do not include aeronautical or hydrographic charts. These charts are used by special forces of the armed services and not by the common soldier. These specialized maps also refer to air currents or to areas of water as much as they do to land features.

ANALYSIS: This is a straightforward, factual theme for a reader interested in the subject. The author begins immediately with a definition of a military map, and then in three paragraphs discusses the three kinds. The development is thus deductive. The details given are sufficient for the reader to know the difference in the maps. No words are lost by the author in giving the details because the purpose of his definition is to give facts, not fancy, but each paragraph should be developed more fully with additional details. The final paragraph is short, but is necessary so that the maps excluded can be mentioned. The whole theme is one of impersonal presentation and is in keeping with the material discussed.

Note that the author undoubtedly used a textbook in military science as his source. Such use of authoritative material is perfectly acceptable, just as long as the student puts the material into his own words.

SAMPLE THEME—ANALYSIS:

Manners Are Important

As one looks about, it becomes very easy to conclude that good manners seem to be a thing of the past. More and more people seem to be discourteous to one another, more indicative of a "survival of the fittest" attitude than of living in a civilized society. Although much of what was considered good manners at the turn of the century may no longer be appropriate, common courtesy and acceptable behavior are still necessary to make life pleasant, especially as our cities become more and more crowded. Although common courtesy is the underlying framework, good manners are manifested in two distinct areas, business and social relationships. Let us look at each of these more closely.

The world of business has become increasingly impersonal over the years. The advent of computers has removed the personal touch from many business dealings. It is not uncommon, when phoning a company, to get a recorded message telling us which number to press. When we finally do get a live person on the other end, he often seems uncaring. Good business sense, though, would dictate the importance of getting back to the personal touch. The speaker should identify himself by name to the caller and make every effort to be courteous and helpful. Above all, he should take great pains to assure the call is not disconnected. In addition, he should make certain that the caller is connected to his party and not kept waiting long while listening to canned music. Good manners will assure happy, loyal customers.

Good manners are, perhaps, most frequently associated with social relationships. Unfortunately, here again they seem to be in decline. The rise of women's liberation has given some people the false impression that good manners are no longer necessary. Holding the door open for another and giving up one's seat on a crowded bus to an elderly person, a pregnant woman, or an obviously tired person seem to be things of the past. People also seem to have forgotten how to behave as an audience. It is not uncommon to see people putting their feet up on the seats in front of them or talking loudly during a movie or play. Even getting to the theater on time and remaining until after the last curtain call are manners no longer adhered to. It seems that it is much more important to be the first one out of the parking lot than to let everyone enjoy the entire show. We won't even talk about courtesy on the road, like giving the other driver the right of way, not cutting someone off, or letting someone merge into one's lane. Even restaurants are not immune from the lack of good manners. Young parents do not seem to care that their children are roaming throughout the restaurant or are crying and disturbing the other guests. Nor do many people have any idea of how to eat in public, for instance, how to use their utensils properly. These examples touch only the surface of the rapid decline of good manners.

Good manners are essential for people to live comfortably with each other. As our cities become more and more crowded, it is the good manners that will make the difference between a civilized society and a jungle. We must all be able to expect certain types of behavior of our fellow denizens or the quality of life will rapidly deteriorate.

ANALYSIS: This theme is in part one of definition, for the writer does tell us both directly and indirectly what he deems to be good manners. However, it is more one of analysis, since he points out in the introduction that good manners are manifested in two areas, business and social relationships, and then proceeds to analyze each area separately in the two body paragraphs. In each paragraph he cites specifics to support his contention that good manners are on the decline and offers suggestions as to what constitutes good manners. His concluding paragraph reinforces his thesis about the importance of manners and their effect.

SAMPLE THEME—LITERARY ANALYSIS:

The writing of literary analyses is a subject unto itself and calls for extended rules, varied techniques, and skills beyond the scope of this book. The following poem and analysis are presented as illustrative of the analysis form, not of the exact way to analyze literature.

A Description of a City Shower

by Jonathan Swift

Careful observers may foretell the hour
(By sure prognostics) when to dread a shower,
While rain depends, the pensive cat gives o'er
Her frolics and pursues her tail no more.
Returning home at night, you'll find the sink   5
Strike your offended sense with double stink.
If you be wise, then go not far to dine;
You'll spend in coach-hire more than save in wine.
A coming shower your shooting corns presage,
Old aches throb, your hollow tooth will rage: 10
Sauntering in coffee-house is Dulman seen;
He damns the climate and complains of spleen.

Meanwhile the South, rising with dabbled wings,
A sable cloud athwart the welkin flings,
That swilled more liquor than it could contain,   15
And, like a drunkard, gives it up again.
Brisk Susan whips her linen from the rope,
While the first drizzling shower is borne aslope:
Such is that sprinkling which some careless quean

Flirts on you from her mop, but not so clean: 20
You fly, invoke the gods; then turning, stop
To rail; she singing, still whirls on her mop.
Not yet the dust had shunned the unequal strife,
But, aided by the wind, fought still for life,
And wafted with its foes by violent gust, 25
'Twas doubtful which was rain and which was dust.
Ah! where must needy poet seek for aid,
When dust and rain at once his coat invade?
Sole coat, where dust cemented by the rain
Erects the nap, and leaves a cloudy stain. 30

Now in contiguous drops the flood comes down,
Threatening with deluge this devoted town.
To shops in crowds the daggled females fly,
Pretend to cheapen goods, but nothing buy.
The Templar spruce, while every spout's abroach, 35
Stays till 'tis fair, yet seems to call a coach,
The tucked-up sempstress walks with hasty strides,
While streams run down her oiled umbrella's sides.
Here various kinds, by various fortunes led,
Commence acquaintance underneath a shed. 40
Triumphant Tories and desponding Whigs
Forget their feuds, and join to save their wigs.
Boxed in a chair the beau impatient sits,
While spouts run clattering o'er the roof by fits,
And ever and anon with frightful din 45
The leather sounds; he trembles from within.
So when Troy chairmen bore the wooden steed,
Pregnant with Greeks impatient to be freed
(Those bully Greeks, who, as the moderns do,
Instead of paying chairmen, run them through), 50
Laocoon struck the outside with his spur,
And each imprisoned hero quaked for fear.

Now from all parts the swelling kennels flow,
And bear their trophies with them as they go:
Filth of all hues and odours seem to tell 55
What street they sailed from, by their sight and smell.
They, as each torrent drives, with rapid force
From Smithfield, or St. Pulchre's shape their course,
And in huge confluence joined at Snow Hill ridge,

Fall from the conduit prone to Holborn Bridge. 60
Sweepings from butchers' stalls, dung, guts, and blood
Drowned puppies, stinking sprats, all drenched in mud
Dead cats and turnip-tops come tumbling down the flood.

An Analysis of "A Description of a City Shower"

On the surface "A Description of a City Shower" is a very colorful and vivid picture of eighteenth-century London immediately before, during, and after a shower. If the reader looks more closely, he finds that Swift is satirizing weather prophets, certain specific types of city characters, heroic poetry, and the filthiness of English towns. The poem consists of four stanzas which describe consecutively the shower's being forecast by certain signs, the shower's initial outburst, the shower's main deluge, and the shower's aftermath.

The first stanza begins by stating that weather can be forecast and gives substantiating examples in the succeeding ten lines. A pensive cat, a stinking sewer, painful corns, and aching tooth, and a complaining hypochondriac are listed as "sure" signs of impending rain. Swift advises the reader in lines 7–8 that dining across town where the wine is cheaper will be impractical should it rain. The loafer in lines 11–12 is representative of many people in eighteenth-century England who felt it stylish to constantly complain of "spleen"—meaning melancholy or low spirits.

In the second stanza the shower's initial outburst stirs up the dust and plasters everything with mud. The rain cloud is alluded to as a drunkard ready to vomit from too much drink.

A housewife retrieves her washing from the line, but not before it is sprinkled with rain. Swift satirized the epic simile in lines 19–22. He uses the transitional word "such" and appropriate epic form, but with degrading and comic intent. In lines 23–26 Swift describes the stirring of dust by the shower's initial sprinkling and wind. Lines 27–30 reveal a "needy" poet with only one coat and it plastered with mud.

The full blast of the shower is described in the third stanza; it causes various reactions in different people. Splattered women pretend to shop, and a lawyer pretends to wait for a coach; both are merely utilizing shelter from the rain. A seamstress with tucked-up skirt wades through the wet streets. To save their wigs, even such bitter political enemies as Tories and Whigs stand together under the same shelter. In lines 43–52 Swift depicts the animosity between noblemen and common servants. By analogy, he refers to a dandy and his chairmen as the Greeks and Trojans in Homer's *Odyssey*. The dandy is frightened by noises because he fears the chair-men may rob or murder him. Swift compares the dandy's fear to that of the Greeks inside the wooden horse at the gates of Troy. The parenthetical matter in lines 49–50 suggests the 18th-century dandy's ill-treatment of his chair-men. Swift again satirizes the epic simile in lines 47–52. He derives his "Troy chairmen," Greeks, and "Laocoon" from the *Odyssey* but again uses Homer's material in a degrading manner.

The fourth stanza, which concerns the aftermath of the shower, paints an unforgettable picture of the city's filthiness. The open gutters with their burdens of waste make a lasting impression upon the reader. The triplet in lines 61–63, with its Alexandrine in line 63, is a satirical jab at heroic prosody. The heroic couplet, the triplet, and the Alexandrine are associated with epics and other heroic poetry. Swift uses these exalted poetic forms but fills them with the filthiest, most offensive subject matter imaginable.

Swift accomplishes at least three things in his poem. He depicts the eighteenth-century English city's physical conditions so well that the reader can almost smell the drains. His epithets very adeptly enhance the reader's conception of the characters in the poem. And finally, he manages some very good satire on heroic prosody, especially in the concluding triplet of the last stanza.

ANALYSIS: In analyzing literature, one of the easiest approaches is to discuss points item by item as they are found in the original, and to merely interpret each point as it is being discussed. Such is the technique found in this essay. The technique is the tried-and-true method used by students for generations. Because it is so conventional, however, many teachers forbid their students to write such an analysis.

Aside from the conventionality, this theme does a good job of interpreting Swift's poem. Note that the poem is relatively clear and direct, with little of the symbolism and imagery one ordinarily finds in poetry. As such, it is easier to interpret than a highly symbolic work.

The paragraphs logically follow the stanzas of the poem. The concluding paragraph is excellent in that it summarizes three things accomplished by Swift and gives evidence of some original thinking and acute observations by the student.

SUGGESTED TOPICS FOR DEFINITION–ANALYSIS THEMES:

1. Sexist attitudes

2. College dropouts

3. A good teacher

4. A well-adjusted person

5. Affirmative action

6. Political correctness

7. Hard metal rock

8. Altruism

9. Promiscuity

10. The modern family

11. Bilingual education

12. Sexual harassment

13. A sense of humor

14. The perfect body

DESCRIPTIVE

Since you are a beginning writer, it is best that you do not try to write a descriptive theme to evoke a response—one in which skillful use of figures of speech, words, details, and tone induces in the reader strong feelings. Instead, since logical, organized, clear writing is your aim, descriptions which are informative are likely to be more successful.

Thus, avoid trying to duplicate the descriptions found in novels, poetry, advertisements, and the like. Instead, strive for the factual, condensed, detailed presentation that you find in textbooks (biology, chemistry, mathematics) or in mail-order catalogs.

With descriptive themes, a preliminary outline is strongly urged. It need not be a formal outline, but merely a list of features which you feel are the main ones. Group like details together, using any logical approach. An automobile, for instance, could be discussed in terms of styling, engine, and performance. Once you have grouped like items, each group will become a paragraph in your theme. If you feel that one group of details is more important, save this paragraph for the end.

APPLICATION: Now study the suggestions and read the list of do's and don't's. Then read the theme, including the analysis given. As you read the theme, refer to the suggestions and the list to see how the theme has implemented them. Once you have a good idea of what to do, look at the suggested list of topics and decide what your topic will be. When you have written your first draft, recheck the suggestions to see if you have included everything.

SUGGESTIONS: The introduction will let the reader know if you are being informative or evoking a response. Most themes do the former. There is no formula for developing a descriptive theme. Suggestions are order of place, order of prominence, order of importance, front to back, and so on. If you are describing a person, consider appearance, habits, gestures, mannerisms, speech, voice, what others say about him, and so on.

Each succeeding paragraph will be devoted to the particular order you have chosen. Use transitions (see DEFINITIONS). Move to another detail in each paragraph. Be sure that each paragraph has a topic sentence or a controlling idea.

Your conclusion could reaffirm your opening statements, or it could be a value judgment. See HOW TO CONCLUDE A THEME for other possible endings.

DO'S AND DON'T'S:

1. Remember that any description (of a person or thing) can have a logical division of presentation. Decide what the main points of interest are. Each of these main points will then have at least one paragraph devoted to it.

2. Descriptive writing, you will note, is developed just as are DEDUCTIVE or INDUCTIVE themes.

3. Describing a thing is much easier than describing a person.

4. Adjectives and figures of speech (similes and metaphors) are very important in descriptions. Remember that your choice of details and your choice of words are a clue to your feelings; they will also provoke a feeling in the reader. Be careful about the connotations of descriptive words.

5. Use concrete, specific wording, not vague, abstract wording. Does a frightened rabbit run, hop, flee, scuttle, scurry, or bound?

6. There is a difference between giving information and evoking a response. The latter is very difficult.

7. Study descriptions given in catalogs, advertisements, and the like, which treat the same thing you are to describe. Note the use of comparatives and superlatives.

8. Remember that most descriptive themes are assigned to test your ability to organize, as well as to test your ability to use figurative language.

9. Avoid clichés. Be careful of the words you use after *like* and *as*. On the other hand, do not wrack your brain trying to write new imagery. Farfetched figures of speech are as bad as trite figures of speech.

10. Note that descriptions written by advertising people are not always grammatically correct. They use the superlative degree when they should use the comparative. They say "This is a better buy!" In your theme, you would have to finish such a sentence by adding "than the other product."

11. Check the PROOFREADING CHART.

SAMPLE THEME—DESCRIPTION:

The Gym

Pandemonium perhaps best describes one's initial impression upon entering the gym. After leaving the sign-in desk that stares out through the all-glass front at the parking lot, I pass through the turnstile at the side of the desk and enter the cavernous main room of the fitness center. I am immediately overwhelmed by a cacophony of noises and a blur of bodies furiously working the machines. The blaring rock-and-roll music from the loudspeakers mingles with the clanging of metal against metal as weights drop against weights. The hum of conversation is frequently interrupted by the heavy breathing and grunting as muscles strain to lift ever heavier weights. I stand there blinking my eyes as if I had just come out of a tunnel into the bright sun. Slowly, things come into focus.

The room I'm in is quite impressive. To my left are two rows of about thirty stationary Life Cycles and recumbent cycles. At right angles to these are four rows of various Nautilus machines stretching at least two hundred feet from one end to the other. These are backed by ten treadmills, which are in constant use. In the far left and far right corners are the Stair-masters, where the more masochistic members spend their time "climbing" at a furious pace to nowhere. Puddles of sweat collect at their feet as proof of their efforts. The grey carpet and the grey walls, decorated with modernistic red and dark-grey striping, lend a somewhat dismal air to the place, which is reinforced by the black ceiling.

I turn to my right and head for the free-weight room, which is readily visible through the glass wall. Here is where the "serious" body builders spend most of their time. The sweat glistening on their bodies is proof of their efforts. Various weight machines are carefully scattered about the room, while the free weights are lined up with military precision according to weight. The whirring of the overhead fans sets the tempo for "pumping iron." The men and women here are the hard bodies that one imagines when thinking of Californians: the skin is taut, the buttocks firm, the muscles rippling. And they take every advantage of admiring their bodies in the full mirrored walls that are on three sides of the room. Only the wall on the left of the entrance is not mirrored. This glass wall looks into the aerobic room.

The pulsing music sets the beat for the step exercise class. The room, approximately the same size as the weight room—about 50 by 125—is bare except for the neon "AEROBIC" sign over the instructor's platform. The hardwood floor reflects the dancers' legs, giving the feeling that another class is dancing on their heads below them. For some reason, mostly women are in this room. Their spandex leotards and thong tights make some men pause between their sets as they stare through the glass wall. But the dancers are oblivious to them. The pulsing beat of the tape player and the encouraging shouts from the instructor, like a drill sergeant counting cadence, keep the class moving in Rockette-like precision steps.

The time has come; I can't delay it any longer. I opt to return to the main gym and use the Stairmaster. My masochistic nature has won out. As I step on the machine and punch in all the appropriate numbers, I promise myself once again that I will get the T-shirt that reads "I Survived the Stairmaster."

ANALYSIS: The opening sentence sets the controlling tone, which the writer reinforces with his diction. Words like *stares*, *cavernous*, *cacophony*, *blaring*, *grey*, and *black* put the reader into a dismal mood. The opening paragraph does not paint a bright, joyous picture.

The overall organization is from general to specific, and the description is presented in spatial order. The first paragraph gives a general overview of the gym. In the next three paragraphs, the writer moves spatially from one room to the other, describing each one from the persona's (the "I") viewpoint. Note how effectively the last sentence in the third paragraph leads the reader into the description of the aerobic room. The last paragraph is a logical explanation of why the writer chose to describe the gym: he was trying to delay the inevitable.

All in all, this is a fairly decent description. The dominant tone is set from the start, the theme is developed in a spatial order, the diction is good in that it reinforces the tone. However, although the writer does use some imagery— "puddles of sweat," "like a drill sergeant counting cadence"—and some onomatopoeia, as in "whirring," "clanging," and "pulsing," more vivid imagery would make this theme more dynamic.

SUGGESTED TOPICS FOR DESCRIPTIVE THEMES:

1. An outdoor paradise

2. A beautiful car

3. A college town

4. What tourists want to see in my home town

5. The new housing project

6. A beautiful vacation spot

7. My home

8. My dormitory room

9. How not to teach

10. My dream husband or wife

11. A good friend

12. My father or mother

FLASHBACK

The flashback is a tried-and-true device to capture the reader's attention. Since the end of (or the reason for) any sequence of events is usually the most interesting, the flashback is used to hint at that end or reason. The flashback, thus, is not a development in itself, but is used in conjunction with other developments.

While the flashback is common in literary presentations—novels, dramas, television programs—it need not be restricted to them. Indeed, it is very often used for expository writing. The illustrative theme "Check Your Equipment" in this section is a valid expository use of the flashback technique. In paragraph four, the generalization "Check your fishing equipment" is followed by the particulars. The theme is thus DEDUCTIVE.

Flashbacks also can be and are used throughout a novel, play, movie, etc. But for a young writer, it is best to restrict its use to the beginning. The one thing to be careful of is that the flashback is not foolish, that it is in keeping with the purpose of the expository writing. In short, a flashback does not have to be literary or dramatic; it can be as matter-of-fact as the remainder of the theme. If it captures the reader's interest without causing him to laugh at the author, it succeeds.

APPLICATION: Now study the suggestions and read the list of do's and don't's. Then read the theme, including the analysis given. As you read the theme, refer to the suggestions and the list to see how the theme has implemented them. Once you have a good idea of what to do, look at the suggested list of topics and decide what your topic will be. When you have written your first draft, recheck the suggestions to see if you have included everything.

SUGGESTIONS: Begin a flashback as close to the conclusion, the effect, as you can. Do not "give the plot away" in the first paragraph, but end the paragraph with a question, with a comment that the remainder of the theme will pertain to the flashback. In a short theme, your flashback should be short, certainly no longer than about one-fourth of your theme.

The succeeding paragraphs will then follow a logical order, usually chronological, step-by-step, or ascending order of importance. In a paper of theme length, the flashback should not be too long, perhaps two paragraphs at the most. It is possible to use reverse chronology all through the paper. See CHRONOLOGICAL form.

In a short theme, you should arrive at where you began your theme in about the fourth paragraph. Then finish your development. You may or may not have a concluding paragraph. In a long paper, you may continue with advice, a discussion of similar things, do's and don't's, and so on.

DO'S AND DON'T'S:

1. Note that the flashback form uses the cause-to-effect form in reverse. That is, all or part of the effect, the result, the conclusion, is given first; then you go back and trace the particulars, usually in chronological order.

2. The flashback technique is used frequently in hunting and fishing articles, adventure stories, how-to-do articles, and the like, as a rhetorical device to capture the reader's interest. It is also a frequent device in television and in the movies.

3. A good way to write a theme using the flashback is to write the theme using one of the usual forms. Then, write the flashback. In other words, you have to know your ending before you can write a flashback which hints at or gives the conclusion.

4. Since the flashback technique often involves action and dialogue, it should be considered for lighter veins, for drama, for literary effectiveness. It is best not to use it

for serious subjects, highly scientific reports, and the like, where the reader's interest is not so much one of literary curiosity as it is in the subject itself. Thus, a report on the cause of the death of fish in a polluted stream would not use the flashback if it were for a scientific journal, but could use it in a popular magazine which sportsmen read.

5. Be sure that your flashback is effective, pertinent, valid, not just thrown in as an "arty" technique.

6. Check the PROOFREADING CHART.

SAMPLE THEME—FLASHBACK:

Check Your Equipment

"No more talking," I whispered to Billy. "Crawl real slow. Don't make any noise. Whatever you do, don't stand up." Billy nodded his head. He knew that it was now or never as well as I did. It was our last chance before striking camp and returning home.

The last twenty yards I covered as cautiously as a soldier crawling across a battlefield. And this was war, war against old "Bucket Head," the name given to the huge bass that had set up his domain in the deep pool at the wide turn of the creek. Dozens of fishermen had tried to catch him; a few had managed to hook him, but the bass had darted around sunken logs and weeds so that the fishermen eventually pulled in a broken line. Now it was my turn. That is why my approach was so cautious. Just a few feet more remained until I reached the safety of the bush which would hide me from view of the bass.

Finally I reached the bush. I stood up slowly, looked to see if Billy was watching, and waved at him. My fly rod was already assembled. Three times I false cast, being careful that the live cricket on my hook would not be pulled off. Then, the final swing of the rod, with just a bit more pressure so that the hook would settle far out near the willow. And that's what undid me: the tip section of my flyrod came loose and went flying to land with a splash in the center of the pool. There went my chance to fool anything. After a splash like that, even the minnows would remain quiet for an hour.

Has something like this ever happened to you? Of course it has. I had planned everything, but I had neglected to check my equipment. I knew that the ferrule on my flyrod was loose, but had kept putting the repair job off. To prevent anything like that happening again, each winter I check all my fishing tackle. Here's what I do.

First I check my rods. I see that all ferrules and guides are on tight. I check the guides to see if grooves are worn in them. If so, I replace them. A worn guide will cause any line to wear thin and eventually break. I also check the windings, applying clear lacquer with a camel-hair brush wherever needed.

Next, I take my reels apart, checking each part for wear. I wash the reel in a coffee can filled with turpentine. Then I apply a light coat of fine oil to the parts and reassemble the reels. The final touch is to apply a drop of clear nail polish on all screws so they can't work loose. I also discard all monofilament lines that I used the previous summer. It costs but a couple of dollars to buy new lines; so why take a chance with a worn line? My silk, nylon, and fly lines I treat according to the manufacturer's instructions.

All my lures and flies are then attended to. I resharpen the hooks of every lure. I touch up all the rusted and worn and chipped spots on the lures. I tighten all screws, check all over to see that nothing can pull loose. I also check the flies thoroughly, applying new hackle and windings applied wherever necessary. I then store the flies in a sealed jar.

Like most fishermen, I do not find the things I do a chore. I spend my happy winter evenings spreading all my fishing gear out and getting everything in shape for another season. You can bet that the next time I sneak up on old Bucket Head, my equipment will be in excellent shape!

ANALYSIS: This is a conventional flashback approach in that the author catches our interest immediately with his use of dialogue and action. The technique is frequently used to add human interest to a how-to-do-it essay. Note that the flash-back covers half the theme, perhaps a bit too long in a theme of five hundred words for the author's purpose of explaining how to keep fishing gear in shape. However, the second half of the theme does give enough information for most purposes. The theme obviously could have omitted the flashback and started immediately to discuss things to do.

The conclusion is appropriate in that it refers to the introduction and ends on a note of human interest.

If we question the use of a flashback for such a theme, we need only to consult the popular magazines devoted to hunting and fishing to find many articles developed using the same technique.

SUGGESTED TOPICS FOR FLASHBACK THEMES:

1. A day I'll never forget

2. A case of mob action

3. Man—nature's worst enemy

4. A sportsman's paradise

5. A loser becomes a winner

6. A tragic mistake

7. Experience pays off

8. I learned the hard way

9. There's more to cooking than recipes

10. Plan before acting

HOW-TO; HOW IT IS DONE

A how-to theme implies that the writer knows how to do what he is discussing, whether it be hunting rabbits, cleaning a chicken, baking bread, or avoiding work. In such a theme the writer not only has to organize his presentation, he should also be correct in his facts. A factual error is as serious as one in grammar.

A how-it-is-done theme can be based upon personal experience or upon research. You may not be a champion swimmer, but if you have watched a champion swimmer in his months and years of practice, you could write a theme on how he became the champion. Similarly, you could be interested in how leather is tanned and do sufficient research to write a competent theme.

Whatever your topic, a step-by-step approach is mandatory. Thus, a preliminary jotting down of the details to be discussed is called for. Facts, details, do's and don't's, cautions, tips, explanations—all are needed and should be itemized before the theme is written. In short, the more care you take before actually writing your theme, the easier the writing will be.

APPLICATION: Now study the suggestions and read the list of do's and don't's. Then read each theme, including the analysis given. As you read each theme, refer to the suggestions and the list to see how the theme has implemented them. Once you have a good idea of what to do, look at the suggested list of topics and decide what your topic will be. When you have written your first draft, recheck the suggestions to see if you have included everything.

SUGGESTIONS: Most how-to themes have a prefatory paragraph which discusses the reasons why the author is writing the paper. A good opening is to ask the reader a question or two. The opening and the development of either how-to or how-it-is-done themes will be similar. Explanations, warnings, hints, do's and don't's, etc., should come where they are needed, not at the conclusion of the theme.

Paragraphs are short. Sentences are short. Clearness and exactness are more important than literary effectiveness or strict adherence to paragraphing, topic sentences, and the like, more so in the how-to theme than in the how-it-is-done theme. But if you can be both stylistic and clear, do so. Most how-to articles list items needed, and so on, at the end. Tell the reader at the beginning that such information is included.

Your conclusion will probably be a formula ending. That is, it will state that if "instructions are followed," the reader will meet with success.

DO'S AND DON'T'S:

1. Remember that a how-to theme demands that the author be an expert. A how-it-is-done theme in most cases will call for research.

2. Determine your audience. For instance, an article on how to make a chest of drawers would be much more detailed and explanatory if it were for novices than if it were for craftsmen.

3. Do remember that logical development is mandatory. Explain things needed as they logically come up. Do not wait until the last paragraph.

4. It is best to set off tables, dimensions, and so on, rather than try to incorporate them in text.

5. In many cases, you also have to say why something is done, not merely how.

6. Do use charts, maps, pictures, illustrations, tables, and so on, which are clearly labeled. The more detailed your paper, the more such material is needed.

7. Do note the techniques used in how-to articles written in the popular magazines.

8. If you are writing a how-to theme, the same demands upon organization, knowledge, and expertness are called for.

9. Do not combine how-to papers with narration, flashbacks, and the like. The essence is clearness and exactness, not literary technique.

10. Do not attempt too big a project for theme purposes. Build a bird house, not a house.

11. Beware of "humorous" how-to themes. Student humor is frequently far short of what is imagined. Irony is not easy to master.

12. Do not forget to include the don't's. That is, warn the reader of the pitfalls, dangers, and so forth, that he will run across.

13. Check the PROOFREADING CHART.

SAMPLE THEME—HOW-TO:

The Art of Writing an "F" Paper

I know that you have had a very difficult time trying to master the art of writing a failing theme. No matter what you tried, you always wound up receiving a passing grade. Not to worry! If you follow the directions I am about to give you, you will not only receive an F on your next theme, you will also be commended by your instructor for your ability to amass so many errors in a single paper.

Your first major project is selecting a topic. Be certain to choose a topic about which you know little or nothing and one that will have no interest whatsoever for your reader. A topic such as "Russian czars and their effect on eating habits" should work fine. Next, don't bother to formulate a thesis, for that may force you to know what it is you want to say. It is much better to try free association. In that way, your reader will find it truly impossible to follow anything you might have to say. To be doubly certain, do not under any circumstances prepare an outline. If, unfortunately, you have been assigned a topic, don't despair. Either take a detour that will allow you to avoid dealing with it directly or, better yet, ignore the assigned topic altogether. You can be assured that will be a definite point in your favor in getting that much desired F.

As any novice writer knows, paragraph organization is an effective means of letting your reader know what each idea is and how it is developed. In writing an F paper you must be certain to avoid effective and accurate paragraphing at all costs. Keep your reader guessing as to when a new idea begins by starting paragraphs at random. A good way is to begin a paragraph whenever you're interrupted, such as when the phone rings or you get a snack. Or you might prefer not to divide your paper into paragraphs at all. Let your reader guess when one idea ends and another begins. Avoid paragraph coherence and unity at all costs. Be sure to keep going off on tangents and to shift your point of view. That should keep the reader guessing. Also avoid logical organization and transition. If you must use any transitional words, be sure to use inaccurate ones. If you say "therefore," be sure it is followed by a contrasting thought. Never follow a "first" with a "second." This is guaranteed to make your reader give up in despair.

Sentence structure, grammar, and mechanics are also essential in writing an F paper. Sprinkle your writing with frequent fragments, run-ons, and awkward constructions. Avoiding complete sentences as often as possible. (That's a good example.) Let your reader guess what you mean when you say "Up the street the soldiers they are marching down." It should take him a while to figure out the meaning. Dangling participles and misplaced modifiers will also aid the confusion. "He shot at the rabbit running across the field with his rifle" will give your reader an interesting mental picture. Of course, don't overlook misspellings: "than" for "then" and "principle" for "principal" are good beginnings. Improper punctuation—or, better yet, no punctuation—incorrect word choice, and ample trite expressions also certainly will go a long way in giving you that F you crave.

There are many additional methods you can employ: padding, avoiding any specific data to support arguments, circular reasoning, fallacious reasoning, omitting a title from your paper, and not writing a conclusion (but be sure to write "The End" at the end). And don't forget to be sloppy. Make sure that there are ample cross-outs in your final draft (better yet, just submit your first draft). Also, write on both sides of the paper; don't leave margins; and be sure to leave some food stains on the paper from your snacks. I assure you after writing an F paper once, you will be able to do it again and again. And you will be the toast of your classmates.

ANALYSIS: Although this is definitely a how-to paper, it is written rather facetiously. The writer takes all the errors that often appear on failing papers and tells the reader that he can accomplish writing such a paper easily. In the opening paragraph, he sets his facetious/sarcastic tone in the first sentence. He then proceeds to devote the three body paragraphs to the three areas of poor writing: topic selection and thesis statement, paragraphing, and sentence structure and mechanics. In each he gives specific examples of how the reader can accomplish this task. The final paragraph suggests some additional methods that can be employed and reiterates that the process outlined will assure the reader of achieving his goal—an F paper. Note that by doing the exact opposite of the advice given, the reader can write a good paper.

SAMPLE THEME—HOW IT IS DONE:

The Big Ones

One of the favorite sayings in the magazines devoted to fishing is the "Ten percent of the fishermen catch ninety percent of the fish." I find nothing to argue about over these figures, for I believe that they are close to the truth. Why is this so? In the following paragraphs, I shall present my opinion on how they do it.

Firstly, real fishermen fish. They are not just once-a-week fishermen. They have the time, the money, and the opportunity to fish which the average fisherman does not have. They are fishing three, four, five times a week; and they are fishing for long stretches of time. With this experience, they get to know the local waters like their kitchens. They also get to know the good and bad spots, the movement of fish, and so on.

Secondly, they have proper equipment. The old cartoon of the barefoot boy with safety-pin hook and a can of worms and a huge string of fish is strictly a "fish story." The experts have proper rods and reels, lines, lures. They also have boats, motors, boots, all kinds of equipment which enable them to spend long, pleasant days at their sport.

Thirdly, the experts fish the waters where the fish are. The typical unsuccessful fisherman spends perhaps a few hours on weekends on the banks of the local reservoir, banks worn bare by the hundreds of other unsuccessful fishermen who walk around it day after day, and with perhaps a hundred speedboats and water skiers churning the water to a soupy mess. The expert is on other waters; he's on the big TVA lakes, or in upper Canada, or in wild and remote areas. He's on the seldom-fished big waters where the big fish are. And, of course, he's there when the fish are biting, not on a hot Sunday afternoon when even the mosquitoes are waiting for the cool evening before biting. Obviously, this big-water fishing takes time and money, something that ninety percent of fishermen do not have.

And finally, the expert has a guide. When he goes off to fish, he has the money to hire a local guide who can take him to the exact spot at the right time with the right lure. The two of them jump into a boat; the guide takes over. After a run to the fishing waters, the guide stops the boat, points, and grunts, "Old line-buster here. Put on number two wobbler, throw out fifty feet, count to ten, and strike hard." The modern guide also has a camera along to take the picture of the expert holding up "old line-buster." It is a "package deal." Many of the advertisements in the sport magazines guarantee results—no fish, no pay.

So there you have my opinion about who catches the fish and how they do it. Of course, becoming an expert fisherman has its drawbacks: it becomes more of a chore than a recreation when one attacks it as a full-time avocation.

ANALYSIS: Note that the author wisely says in his first paragraph that his discussion is "my own opinion." However, this is not good style. He should have stated that last sentence differently. He could, in other words, be wrong about how big fish are caught, but his theories stand correct until disproved.

The development is DEDUCTIVE, with the thesis being how ten percent of the fishermen catch ninety percent of the fish. Then, paragraphs two, three, four, and five discuss in turn the author's four contentions. The discussion is quite logical, so much so that the reader has a strong feeling that the author knows what he is talking about.

Note that since we have the feeling that the author is a bit bitter, he wisely concludes his theme on the reflective note that he will take his chances as ninety percent of the fishermen do and that he will, as a consequence, still enjoy fishing.

SUGGESTED TOPICS FOR HOW-TO AND HOW-IT-IS-DONE THEMES:

1. How to change a tire

2. Making a dress

3. The art of being popular

4. Getting ahead in school

5. How to study for an exam

6. How to remain single

7. How to be expelled

8. Building a conference champion

9. Raising crops

10. Teaching your dog to obey

11. How to look alert in class when bored

12. Building a tree house

13. Cake baking made easy

14. How to lose friends

15. How to shower without hot water

16. Steel making (needs research)

17. Tanning leather (needs research)

18. How an assembly line works (needs research)

19. How to get along with obnoxious people

20. How to enjoy an opera

IMITATIVE

In imitating an author's style, one must study his mannerisms, vocabulary, sentence structure, tone, subject matter, and so on. Those authors with a pronounced style—Hemingway, Poe, Mencken, and the like—are easily imitated, but we must remember that they were masters of their trade. Do not attempt to pattern your style after them in everything you write. It is amusing and interesting to try to write like an admired author, but an essay patterned after another's style should be attempted only as an exercise.

It is much easier to imitate a type—a fable, parable, "twist ending" (O. Henry's device), "stream of consciousness" (James Joyce's device), and so on. Here, all one has to do is follow the technique of the model. A fable or a parable thus will have a moral, a twist ending will surprise the reader in concluding in an unexpected way, and a stream of consciousness will involve putting one's thoughts on paper.

Remember that no matter what imitation you attempt, your theme should be grammatically correct, organized, logical, unified. It is still a theme to be evaluated, not a literary production to be admired.

APPLICATION: Now study the suggestions and read the list of do's and don't's. Then read each theme, including the analysis given. As you read each theme, refer to the suggestions and the list to see how the theme has implemented them. Once you have a good idea of what to do, look at the suggested list of topics and decide what your topic will be. When you have written your first draft, recheck the suggestions to see if you have included everything.

SUGGESTIONS: The development of an imitation theme will follow that of your model. Usually, imitations are of fiction and of poetry, not of expository writing. Note that rigid rules of paragraphing, called for by the rules of expository writing, are not always followed by professional writers, who paragraph more by instinct and for stylistic reasons. Do not try to have a topic sentence for each paragraph unless your model has one.

Note that conclusions are not tidy "wrap-ups." Professional writers avoid formula endings. Their endings fit their style.

DO'S AND DON'T'S:

1. Check with your teacher before writing an imitation or a parody of the work of a professional.

2. Remember that imitating another does not justify your making mistakes in the mechanics.

3. Most imitations take the form of a parody. If you are a novice writer, it is best to stick to those authors whose style is quite obvious: Poe, Hemingway, James, Twain, and the like.

4. Also remember that clever parodies have probably also been done before by other students. In short, do not expect that your cleverness will astound your reader.

5. "Slanting" is imitative. A slanted article is one written after you study the publication you wish to accept your work. You follow the rules, length, style, type of writing, etc., of the publication you are interested in.

6. Don't assume that vocabulary is sufficient to produce an imitation. Sentence length; the rhythm, variety, and kinds of sentences; verbs, adjectives, placement of modifiers; figures of speech, tone, mood, subject matter—a host of things determine an author's style.

7. Don't try to mold your own style to another's style. It is good for beginning writers to admire and study the work of a professional, but slavish imitation is never the route to developing your own individual approach.

8. If you cannot imitate another's style of writing, you could try to imitate a type of writing or speaking—fable, a sermon, a sales "pitch," a carnival barker, or a tour guide's memorized speech. Ordinarily, in this type of writing, you will state in your first paragraph what you are doing.

9. Check the PROOFREADING CHART.

SAMPLE THEME—IMITATIVE OF EDGAR ALLAN POE:

Naomi

I find myself recalling the vision of a girl I knew in the seemingly roseate days of my youth. I think of her so often that at times the thoughts are as joys unknown; and then again, the thoughts I have of her are tinged with melancholy.

She was Naomi. I recall her now as a dream shimmering faintly upon the lake of pleasant reveries. I seem to sense her hand reach out for me and to hear her voice call out to me through the mists that cloud the years. Faintly and hauntingly, the call beats through my mind as if it were a drum of some jungle madness. Naomi! Naomi! Naomi!

She was the breath of life, the song of summer nights, the sob of winds, and the pain of lost love to me. She was my seasons; she was my years. She was all that was all to me; she was all that was not for me.

She was a long journey. She was like going home. She was like leaving home forever. She was nights spent in dreaming and days spent in doing. She was a word, a thought, a cry, a laugh, a walk through green fields, a wind-blown, tree-topped hill.

She was music dancing on flowers and love playing blindman's-buff with fate. She was all that mattered to me. She was all that I wished for and all that I longed for.

Then one day she stole away from me as a wraith at twilight, softly, with no word save a laugh echoing mockingly on the vibrant air.

Now she is gone forever. Nothings remains but the heart of me, a memory that will not die until at last the blessed sleep descends.

ANALYSIS: This theme succeeds not so much because it is an accurate imitation of Poe's style, but because in comparison with the usual theme on a conventional topic which the instructor must read, it is a different, fresh, "literary" theme. To be sure, some of the elements of Poe's style are present: word choice, tone, mood, figures of speech. And the theme of the loss of a loved one is, of course, one of Poe's favorite topics.

Note that the paragraphing is not based upon the use of topic sentences, nor does it follow Poe's style. Rather, each paragraph is a grouping of images into short, manageable length. The short paragraphs give us an opportunity to pause before continuing to read what is essentially a long series of figures of speech—much the same pause that we make in reading stanzas in poetry.

SAMPLE THEME—IMITATIVE OF A TYPE:

A Fable of Moderns, or How Geometry Got One of Its Rules

Once upon a time there lived an exceedingly brave and handsome Indian warrior. Not only did he govern his tribe well, but he also was an excellent leader on the field of battle. Accordingly, he was frequently away fighting.

It so happened that while he was away on a particularly long excursion, his three wives all had babies. In a manner which would be fitting for so great a warrior, the three wives decided to do something special for the chief when he arrived home.

At length, news came back that the successful band of warriors was approaching. The three wives stirred themselves, put on their best attire, and each displayed her offspring on an animal outside the tepee. The first wife placed her baby on a buffalo hide. The second wife placed her baby on a horse hide. The third wife, since she had twins, decided that something more ornate was called for, and so she placed her twins on a hippopotamus hide.

Soon the band of warriors arrived. The handsome and brave chief was the last to enter the village. As was his custom, he did not talk, did not display any emotion. He let the lesser warriors do the bragging and telling of their heroic exploits. The three wives, knowing their husband well, patiently sat on their hides, their babies at their side, on display for their lord and master.

The chief walked slowly along the line of hides. He looked at the first baby and grunted. He looked at the second baby and grunted. The third hide, however, with its twins, caused him to pause. Slowly, his eyes moved from baby to baby. At length he turned to his assistants and commented: "Ugh! The sons of the squaw of the hippopotamus are equal to the sons of the squaws of the two hides."

ANALYSIS: This imitation of a type is much easier to write than is the imitation of a style that we find in the previous theme. In short, imitating a kind or type of prose is not so much an imitation as it is a form of development.

As a fable, the theme succeeds: it uses the conventional introduction-story-moral method we expect; it also succeeds because of the novelty (perhaps a bit strained) of the fable told. Obviously, the author did not write an original fable, but one of the elements of a fable is the implication that it is a retelling of a story. The success of this theme, of course, depends upon our willingness to accept the "punch line." Whether we do or not, however, the student has written a good fable, although a fable generally uses personified animals.

SUGGESTED IMITATIVE TOPICS AND STYLES:

1. Poe's use of mood and tone

2. Hemingway's terse style

3. Franklin's "almanac" style

4. "Purple prose"

5. "Stream of consciousness" style of Woolf or Joyce

6. The style of *Time* magazine

7. Browning's dramatic monologues

8. Francis Bacon's compact essay style

9. Edgar Lee Master's soliloquy style

10. Biblical style

IMPLIED

Since teachers of composition are quite firm in their insistence that themes be organized with a definite thesis sentence and with each paragraph having a topic sentence, a theme with an implied thesis should be avoided unless you first check with your teacher.

The dangers of using an implied thesis are that the reader may get an entirely different implication from that intended, or that two or more implications can easily be drawn from the reading, or that no implication at all can be drawn. One of the major errors made by young writers is that of lack of focus; a series of sentences may ramble on without saying anything in particular or without arriving at a logical conclusion. Unless your implication is very obvious, do not write such a theme. If you decide to write such a theme, read it to a fellow student and ask him what the thesis is. If he does not immediately know, rewrite the theme using a stated thesis.

APPLICATION: Now study the suggestions and read the list of do's and don't's. Then read the theme, including the analysis given. As you read the theme, refer to the suggestions and the list to see how the theme has implemented them. Once you have a good idea of what to do, look at the suggested list of topics and decide what your topic will be. When you have written your first draft, recheck the suggestions to see if you have included everything.

SUGGESTIONS: Since the generalization you are writing about is not stated in an implied theme, your development begins immediately. Each paragraph will be another point which should inescapably lead the reader to come to the same conclusion you have in mind.

Each paragraph should "build your case" without so stating. Do not weakly hint what your generalization is. Either state it (DEDUCTIVE form) or make sure that your thesis is obviously apparent. Ending each paragraph with a question for the reader to answer is a very good way to make your implication stronger.

At the end of the theme the reader is left to draw his own conclusion. End with a question, such as "When are we going to wake up?" or "What are we going to do about this?"

DO'S AND DON'T'S:

1. For novice writers, implied generalizations are dangerous. Unless you know what you are about, it is better to use a form where you definitely state your thesis.

2. Use many questions, but let the reader formulate his own answer. End each paragraph with a question.

3. Implied writings are frequently ironical pieces. The danger of using irony is twofold: you may not make irony clear; and, no matter how clear, many readers never "get the point" and thus the irony has the opposite effect from what you intended.

4. Note that many "low-key" advertisements make their point, not by telling you to buy, but by so describing the value, merit, enjoyment, and security of the product that the implication about which product you should buy is obvious. Thus word choice and tone are extremely important in this kind of writing.

5. Do not write a theme with an implied moral, point, or subject, unless your teacher is first consulted.

6. Be sure that the implication which seems obvious to you will also be obvious to your reader.

7. Consider using either the deductive or the inductive form. Is your intended implied approach better?

8. Do not "give your plot away" in the title.

9. Check the PROOFREADING CHART.

SAMPLE THEME—IMPLIED THESIS:

Teaching Is a Snap

There are those who think that teaching high school students is difficult, but they are wrong. Teaching is perhaps the easiest way to earn a buck there is. After all, how hard can it be to face five classes of totally bored and uninterested students every day? Their sole concern is to avoid being called upon and to survive until the bell signals the end of the period.

It is the students' attitude that makes teaching so easy. Most of them have no desire to learn, especially something as dull and routine as English. For most of them, English is their native tongue and they already talks good, so there ain't much that they can be taught. Also, they don't present a discipline problem. During the first two periods, they are still too sleepy to create too much of a disturbance. For the next two periods, they are getting too hungry and are constantly thinking about lunch and how they will sneak out of school. After lunch, they are too logy from all that food, and before you know it, the last period is devoted to watching the clock so they can get out of school quickly. If one adds to all of this that these youngsters are the television generation—placid blobs, couch potatoes—who are not accustomed to interacting, the teacher does not have to prepare too much or worry about any questions coming from the students. The only disadvantage for the students is that they do not have a remote control, but they do manage to "turn the teacher off" anyway.

The students are also kind enough to make the teacher's work load easier. Even though an English teacher may have as many as 175 students, he need not worry about having too many papers to grade. First of all, as many as seventy-five of these students won't show at any given time. Of those who do come to class, probably half will be unprepared. This effectively reduces the paper load. Second of all, many of those who do submit their papers do so improperly, necessitating that the teacher return them for rewrites. And then, of course, there are those students who feel that having to write in writing courses is a total waste of their time.

Even if the teacher is assigned to one of the more difficult schools, his job is still easy. Some students may bring knives and guns to school, but violence will be directed at other students, and usually not in the classroom. Any conflict between gang members in the class can usually be delayed until school is out. And most of the extortion does not take place in the room itself. So the teacher has it pretty easy.

Of course, there are those few misguided souls who maintain that teaching is one of the most emotionally trying professions. According to them, teachers must carefully prepare lessons so that they can stimulate students with diverse abilities and make them anxious to learn. They must juggle as many as forty different students at any given time who may have many emotional problems. They must motivate students to do their work to the best of their abilities. They must counsel students and at times control the violence that has become part of many of our schools. But these people are misguided, for it has been pointed out, the teachers' lot is an easy one, especially when one considers that they work only half a day, and have all those breaks during the year, as well as two months of vacation every summer. Yes, teaching is a snap.

ANALYSIS: The writer has written a satirical essay and lets the alert reader know from the start that the title is the antithesis. The opening sentence is the real thesis, although the writer maintains it is not which he reinforces in the concluding paragraph. The phrase "earn a buck" further hints at this.

Even though the writer states reasons why teaching is so easy, the astute reader realizes throughout that the exact opposite is intended. Should the reader have any doubts, the last paragraph makes it rather obvious what difficulties confront the teacher on a daily basis. However, in an implied theme there is always the distinct possibility that some readers may miss the irony and sarcasm and take the statements at face value, as did many readers of Swift's "A Modest Proposal." If you are writing for a group that you feel may not be able to infer your thesis, stay away from the implied theme.

SUGGESTED TOPICS FOR IMPLIED THEMES:

1. Should America permit unlimited immigration?

2. Our polluted waters

3. Strip mining havoc

4. The school paper—spokesman for whom?

5. Gun laws

6. Are we mice or men?

7. Open borders

8. "It's for your own good."

9. Buy now; pay forever

10. This is culture?

11. Who owns us?

12. My country, right or wrong

13. This is teaching?

14. This is living?

15. The American justice system

INDUCTIVE

The inductive form of development is just the opposite of the deductive form (turn to the DEDUCTIVE section and read the introductory remarks). In the inductive form, you save the generalization for the end. A child who says "Because you're mean and nasty, I don't like you!" is using an inductive form: the particulars "mean and nasty" lead to the generalization "I don't like you!" Any group of statements which leads to a generalization which can be made about them is in essence an inductive development.

Practically any deductive theme can be made into an inductive one. For instance, turn to the discussion "TO THE STUDENT" at the front of this book. Note that the deductive theme presented there could easily be made inductive by omitting the generalization in the first paragraph—"My three guns are all I need to hunt in this area"—and by placing it in the final paragraph.

If you are in doubt about "saving for the end" any generalization you might make, note in the list of do's and don't's the kinds of topics for which the form is best suited.

APPLICATION: Now study the suggestions and read the list of do's and don't's. Then read the theme, including the analysis given. As you read the theme, refer to the suggestions and the list to see how the theme has implemented them. Once you have a good idea of what to do, look at the suggested list of topics and decide what your topic will be. When you have written your first draft, recheck the suggestions to see if you have included everything.

SUGGESTIONS: Do not state the thesis of an inductive theme or "give the plot away" until your last paragraph. If you must, then see DEDUCTIVE form. You can hint, suggest that the conclusion will be different, amusing, or the like, if the facts or points you are to present so justify. Your introduction, however, must be valid, not just a series of idle remarks.

Each particular will probably have a separate paragraph, though it is possible to discuss more than one particular in any one paragraph, or to discuss a particular in more than one paragraph. Arrange your particulars in a logical order: chronological, ascending importance, and so on. It is the usual practice to save the most important point for the next-to-last paragraph position.

The conclusion, generalization, or thesis is stated in the final paragraph. The above points should inescapably lead to this conclusion. See also DEDUCTIVE and IMPLIED sections.

DO'S AND DON'T'S:

1. Check to see if the DEDUCTIVE form would not be a better presentation.

2. Make sure the points presented justify the conclusion you come to.

3. Remember that inductive writing usually gives only probability, not certainty.

4. Check words like *always*, *all*, *everyone*. It is usually better to use qualifying words (See DEFINITIONS). See also "Title" on PROOFREADING CHART.

5. Save the topic sentence until the end.

6. The inductive form is used for fables, parables, proclamations, edicts, detective stories, morals, generalizations, scientific reports, and the like. Any paper which presents a series of points and concludes with words like *therefore*, *thus*, *and so*, and the like, is an inductive form.

7. Remember that the inductive form is "scientific"—reasoning which by observing something to be true in numerous similar circumstances, concludes that it will be true in all similar circumstances.

8. Define any terms which will clarify your meaning.

9. Arrange your points in increasing (ascending) order of importance, proof, weight, etc.

10. Do not ignore exceptions or facts which an opponent would point out.

11. Do not take for granted that everyone will agree with your particulars. You need facts, figures, charts, authorities, and so on, to back your points.

12. Remember that since inductive generalizations are not determined in advance, they are made only when the accumulated evidence justifies them.

13. Do not use analogies as proof. Analogies are rhetorical devices to clarify, not justify. See ANALOGY section.

14. Check the PROOFREADING CHART.

SAMPLE THEME—INDUCTIVE:

A New Experience

Only five days after we had arrived from Germany, my mother took me to P.S. 16 in our new neighborhood, Williamsburg, in Brooklyn, and enrolled me in school. The dilapidated old building, which I later learned dated from the Civil War, was overwhelming. After a brief discussion with the assistant principal, carried on in a mixture of German and Yiddish, my mother left me to go to work. Here I was, eight years old, unable to speak or understand a word of English, seemingly abandoned in a strange environment.

The assistant principal, a kind, matronly woman, took me by the hand and led me through a series of connected rooms until we reached Mrs. Levy's classroom. A few quick words and she left. There I was in a first-grade class feeling completely ill at ease. The kids stared at me, at this gangling kid too big for the seat who could speak only German. I felt completely lost until Mrs. Levy came over to me with her warm, compassionate smile, and her broken high school German made me feel at ease.

The next few weeks passed rather rapidly. Mrs. Levy spent her lunch hours and recess with me, helping me to learn this new language. Her warmth and genuine concern soon made me feel comfortable in my new surroundings. And her sensitivity and interest in me made me want to keep going to school and learn the language and customs of my newly adopted country. By the time the school year ended two months later, I had somehow learned to speak and read English sufficiently well to be promoted to the fourth grade.

At that time bilingual education was not available. I was thrown into an all-English-speaking situation and forced by circumstances to learn the language. I had to learn enough words in those first few days and weeks to be able to communicate. I doubt if I could have learned English as quickly had I first been taught in my native tongue. To this day, I am convinced that total immersion in an English-speaking environment is the way to go. Bilingual education does not foster mastery of English.

ANALYSIS: This theme is essentially an anecdote in which the writer recalls an event from childhood. As in most anecdotes, the thesis can be inferred from the information presented. However, when the anecdote is used in expository writing, the thesis is usually stated either at the beginning or at the end. Since this is an inductive theme, the writer stated his thesis in the conclusion: "Bilingual education does not foster mastery of English."

SUGGESTED TOPICS FOR INDUCTIVE THEMES:

1. A truth I learned

2. The person I married

3. A student's proclamation

4. A modern fable

5. Automobile insurance

6. Lose a friend

7. How to learn the hard way

8. The best bargain

9. "And so I say to you..."

10. A new truth?

11. Who killed our morale?

12. A student manifesto

13. I should have listened

SPACE FILLER

The term "space filler" has been applied to this section as a deliberate warning to the student writing without a definitely stated thesis. (See also the IMPLIED section.) The term is perhaps unfair, because many famous writers have written and are writing daily, weekly, or monthly columns of a space-filler nature which are highly respected and read by millions. The columns can be found in all the better newspapers and magazines.

However, since you are taking a course where expository writing is expected, you should remember that exposition means an organized, logical, unified, coherent setting forth of a thesis which expounds, explains, or appraises analytically. In short, your theme should talk about one thing, and each and every paragraph in the theme should be directly and unmistakably related to that one thing.

If you insist, however, that you have three or four interesting items for a theme, then relate them to each other. If they are amusing, interesting, a commentary upon the times, or the like, devise a thesis which states the area the items will cover and write the theme using one of the standard forms of development—perhaps INDUCTIVE, DEDUCTIVE, COMPARE AND CONTRAST, or CLASSIFICATION.

APPLICATION: Now study the suggestions and read the list of do's and don't's. Then read the theme, including the analysis given. As you read the theme, refer to the suggestions and the list to see how the theme has implemented them. Once you see how easy it is to have a thesis sentence, you will not make the mistake of stringing an unrelated group of paragraphs together.

SUGGESTIONS: The introduction states or implies that what follows is a miscellaneous "clean up the desk" collection. The tone is light, half apologetic. Frequently such essays are printed with double spacing between items, or some sort of printer's mark between items to signify that they are not related. If the items are related, judicious use of transitions and topic sentences could readily make the selections into a theme.

There is no particular order of presentation. The most important or interesting could come first, in the middle, or last. Present the items in the order which seems most logical if they are related to one another in any logical way. For example, item two may or may not be related to the above or following topics. Conclusions vary widely. There may be none. It may be a half-hearted apology. Space limitations usually dictate the kind and extent of concluding remarks.

DO'S AND DON'T'S:

1. Do not write this type of paper unless you have first checked with your teacher. It is appropriate for human-interest and sports columns found in magazines and newspapers. It is not appropriate for purposes of developing skills in organizing class themes, nor is it appropriate for essay examinations.

2. Usually space fillers do have a controlling idea, perhaps one of humorous signs seen while driving, or one dealing with typographical errors, and the like. As such, they are following the DEDUCTIVE form. Such a development is acceptable for themes if the thesis is stated and if judicious use of transitions ties the ideas together.

3. When written by professionals, space fillers are interesting and may have many regular readers, many of whom contribute material to the authors. The form, however, is best reserved for professionals.

4. Note how the illustrative space filler could easily be made into an acceptable theme by having a thesis sentence in

the first paragraph and by introducing each series of particulars in a regular paragraph fashion.

5. Check the PROOFREADING CHART.

SAMPLE THEME—SPACE FILLER:

Those Words Again

So many letters have come in regarding our discussion in the last issue that we thought we would print some of the more interesting ones.

* * *

Mrs. L. D. Smith of Peoria asks how many of our readers could pronounce the following words correctly: impious, worsted, err, diaper, threepenny, Cairo, Illinois (both words!), Percy Bysshe Shelley, and Cholmondeley (tricky!).

* * *

Roger Jones of Chicago asks which of the following words are spelled correctly: supercede, harrass, repellant, embarass, picnicking, exagerrate, accomodate, sacreligious, seperate (watch it, proofreader!).

* * *

Bill MacAdams of Gary writes in to say that Macadamized comes from four languages: Mac from Gaelic, dam from Hebrew, iz from French, and ed from English.

* * *

Mary Burns of Toledo comments that to call a man a pagan, heathen, and barbarian really means that he lives in the provinces on a heath and wears a beard.

* * *

And finally, we do not apologize for the following puns. We think that they are the best of a lot of really bad ones. Barney

Rich (no address) writes to ask if we have heard about the midget who escaped from Czechoslovakia and roamed about in Europe asking if anyone could cache a small Czech. Ernest Caldwell of Tulsa writes to tell us of a rancher who left his ranch to his sons and named it Focus because it is where the sons raise meet (Ugh!). And Dick Crane of Detroit tells us that the local police threatened to close a burlesque theater because of the suggestive advertising, and so the management put up a new sign: "Hear the Belles Peel."

* * *

Should we continue next week, or have our readers had enough?

ANALYSIS: This is a typical collection of items for a space-filler column in a newspaper or a magazine. Because space available frequently varies from issue to issue, the writer of a space-filler column is forced to use short unrelated items or a series of unrelated items so that one or two can be left out without destroying the continuity of the article. Note that any of the items in this selection could be omitted without harm. If it were the usual thesis-and-topic-sentence, of course, omission of one or more paragraphs could leave either a confused topic or an insufficiently developed topic.

SUMMARY

In most cases, a summary is assigned so that the student can gain experience in selecting and presenting essential information found in a piece of writing. The student, of course, does this constantly in his studying and note taking. Also in library assignments, term papers, and under the pressure of time, the student frequently must condense pages of information for transfer to note cards or into his own personal notes. Obviously, to be of value, the condensation must accurately reflect the meaning of the original.

In most cases, your teacher will give instruction as to the kind and length of summary he wants. If not, remember that writers follow the same procedure in writing that you do: they use a thesis sentence; they use topic sentences in their paragraphing; they frequently repeat key ideas; they themselves summarize what they have said, usually at the end of paragraphs, sections, or the article. In short, the writing to be summarized will have a line of development with which you are familiar. Seek out these key ideas and write them down. Then, reread the selection to see if you have accurately captured the intent, purpose, and meaning of the original. You frequently may use the author's own words, or you may write his ideas in your own words.

Do not try to duplicate the paragraphing of the original. Instead, break down the information into easily managed units. Keep like ideas together, and the paragraphing will take care of itself.

You are, of course, expected to be grammatically correct. Accordingly, be sure to check the PROOFREADING CHART found in the Appendix of this book.

SUGGESTIONS: The development of a summary theme follows that of the source. If you do a thorough job, your paragraphing will take care of itself. Ordinarily, closely related ideas will be in one paragraph. Then, when the source changes to another major topic, you also can start a new paragraph.

It is not necessary to devote one paragraph to one idea. Depending upon the length of your source, one paragraph may well summarize two, three, or even dozens of paragraphs or pages of your source. Since you will have many ideas in brief form, short paragraphs will be easier to handle (and read later on) than long ones. In a summary, you do not add your own conclusion. When you have finished summarizing your source, stop.

DO'S AND DON'T'S:

1. Remember that the purpose of a summary is to select the main points from long selections. A summary is a brief presentation of the material of longer papers, essays, chapters, books, and the like.

2. Summaries vary widely. Check with your teacher for further specific suggestions if the do's and don't's in this list seem to be too detailed.

3. Keep in mind that a summary of theme length will be of an original that is probably at least three or four times longer. The longer the writing which is summarized, the less proportion you will give each point.

4. Thus, depending upon your purpose or your assignment, a summary of a novel could be a sentence or two, a paragraph, a theme, or a paper which is pages in length.

5. Do not summarize paragraph for paragraph. Perhaps as many as a dozen paragraphs of the original could be stated in one paragraph.

6. In general, give as much proportion in your summary as your original gives. A long illustration of a single point, of course, does not need proportionate space in your summary.

7. Read all of the original before deciding your approach. You will thus gain an idea of how much proportion each point will have.

8. The book you are now reading is a summary, a shortened form of the information to be found in books many hundreds of pages in length.

9. Don't paraphrase unless directed to. A paraphrase is a statement in your own words of what another has said. A paraphrase will be almost as long as the original.

10. Unless directed to, don't use your own interpretation, mood, opinion. Keep the meaning, intention, stress, and importance that you find in your source.

11. Avoid saying "The author says." A summary implies that someone else says it.

12. Don't slavishly use the author's words. You may select a word or phrase from the original, but in general do not quote extensively.

13. Don't misinterpret the original in your effort to be concise. Also do not omit minor points which must be

considered in relation to the major points. This generalization is particularly valid if you are to put the summary aside for weeks or months before using it again.

14. Many of the points given above are for summaries which are to be handed to the teacher. For your own purposes, a summary which has the main points of the original stated clearly and logically is all that is demanded.

15. Check the PROOFREADING CHART.

SAMPLE THEME—SUMMARY:

A Summary of the Rules for Comma Usage

When main clauses are joined by the coordinating conjunctions (and, but, for, or, nor), use a comma. The three exceptions are these: 1) When the main clauses are short, a comma is not needed. Example: It was raining but I don't mind. 2) When the subject remains the same, no comma is needed. Example: I walked across the campus last night and I noticed that the lights were out. 3) When the main clauses have internal punctuation, separate the main clauses by a semicolon. Example: I noticed her dress, of course, but did not say anything; and I also noticed her jewelry, about which I had plenty to say.

When a long phrase or an adverb clause precedes the main clause, follow it with a comma. If you will notice this sentence and the preceding one, you will see the rule illustrated. An exception is made to this rule when the introductory phrase or clause is short. Example: When it rains I stay home.

Items in series are separated by commas. Examples: I was tired, cold, and hungry. He ran into the house, down the stairs, and into the coal bin. He said that he was leaving, that he did not care what she did, and that he would never call again. Red, white, and blue are the colors of our flag.

Miscellaneous uses of the comma include the following examples: You, Bill Brown, are lazy (direct address). Bill Brown, who is lazy, will not be elected (adjective clauses—

nonrestrictive). Bill, our captain, was told to leave the game (nouns in apposition). He lives at 17 Oak Lane, Chicago, Illinois (addresses). On May 17, 1929, he was found dead (dates). You are, on the whole, a good student (parenthetical phrase). Seeing that he was cold, I fed him warm soup (participle phrase).

Use a comma when it will prevent misreading. Examples: He cried, for his mother had left. Outside, the house was cheerful looking.

ANALYSIS: This selection adequately summarizes the traditional rules for commas. It has the brief versions of the rules and also wisely gives examples for both the rules and the exceptions. Note that a further reduction could be made by merely using the first sentence of each of the five paragraphs.

The paragraphing, of course, is simply taken care of by using one rule per paragraph. Note that neither an introduction nor a conclusion is needed.

If you wish to compare this summary with a full discussion of comma rules, consult any of the handbooks listed in the Bibliography at the end of this book.

SAMPLE THEME—SUMMARY:

A Summary of Edgar Allan Poe's "The Cask of Amontillado"

Fortunato had injured me often, but when he insulted me I vowed revenge. I did not threaten him but continued to smile in his face. He had one weakness—connoisseurship in wine—and this weakness I would use for my revenge. So, during the carnival season I arranged to meet Fortunato when he was dressed in carnival clothing and nearly drunk with celebrating. I told him that I had bought a cask of Amontillado, but that I wanted an expert like Fortunato or Luchesi to come and taste it to see if I had gotten Amontillado or a cheap substitute. Fortunato, of course, fancied himself an authority and considered Luchesi a fraud; so I knew I had him. I also protested that it was carnival time, that Fortunato was enjoying himself, that the vaults where the wine was stored were cold and damp; but by playing on his vanity, I got him to accompany me.

My palazzo I knew was empty, for I had ordered my servants not to leave; but being servants, they had fled as soon as my back was turned. I got down two flambeaux and gave one to Fortunato. We proceeded to the vaults down long, winding stairs, and finally reached the catacombs of my ancestors, the Montresors, which were below my palazzo. I warned Fortunato to be careful and suggested to him that we go no farther because his cough grew worse in the dampness, and that since he was such an important man, his death would be a blow. This play on his vanity only insured his following me. I broke off the neck of a bottle of wine and gave it to him to allay his cough, knowing that it would further intoxicate him. We drank to the bodies reposing in the catacombs.

Farther and farther we went, past many bones, casks, and finally directly beneath the river where the moisture was trickling down the walls. Again I suggested that we turn back, again he refused, again we drank another bottle of wine. He then made a motion that I did not understand. It turned out that it was a secret gesture used by the society of Freemasons. When Fortunato doubted that I was a member, I withdrew a trowel from beneath my cloak as proof—the significance and the irony of the trowel was lost on him.

Deeper we went into the vaults, finally arriving at a deep crypt. The damp, foul air caused our flambeaux to flicker. Bones were everywhere, even piled high along three walls. The fourth wall had been cleared of bones to reveal a recess four feet deep, three wide, and six or seven high. It was so dark in the recess that we could not see in. I tempted Fortunato by saying that the cask of wine was in the recess, but that perhaps Luchesi... Fortunato called Luchesi an ignoramus and stepped into the recess. I followed him, and before he could recover his wits, I had secured him about the waist with a lock and chain which I then fastened to two staples secured in the wall.

Now that he was mine, I played with him. I suggested that since he didn't want to return to the streets, I must then leave him. He demanded to see the wine, but I produced a quantity of stones and mortar and began to wall up the entrance. Fortunato sobered very quickly. He moaned, shook the chain. I paused to enjoy his terror. When I had bricked in the wall about halfway, I paused to look at him. He screamed, and for a moment I determined to leap in and stab him. Instead, I restrained myself and joined in with his screams as I continued my work. Finally, but one stone remained. Fortunato gave a low laugh, a laugh which made my hair stand on end. He laughed again, said it was a good joke that I was playing on him, that all would laugh when they heard of it, and then suggested we return to the street. "Yes," I said, "let us be gone." "For the love of God, Montresor!" he answered. "Yes," I said, "for the love of God!" He did not reply. Twice I called his name, but all I could hear was the jingling of the chains. My heart grew sick because of the dampness, and so I hurried to force the last stone into place and plaster it. Then I pushed the bones against it. For half a century, no mortal has disturbed the bones. May Fortunato rest in peace!

ANALYSIS: This is a rather lengthy summary of the original story because the author wishes to include most of Poe's details. The summary could easily be cut in half, or a summary of one short paragraph would serve to refresh one's memory. The length of the summary depends upon the usage the student wishes to put it to.

The paragraphing does not follow the original, but is essentially a matter of breaking up the original story into five sections. The student could have used perhaps eight, nine, or ten paragraphs. Since stories are not written like a theme—stories do not use a topic sentence per paragraph—it is up to the one doing the summarizing to break up his theme into convenient sections.

Note that the student does not add his personal comments in the summary. For his own use, of course, any personal comments would add to the value of the summary when he came to use it later on.

SUGGESTED ITEMS TO SUMMARIZE: Ordinarily your teacher will assign a selection to be summarized. If not, then the following would be good practice:

1. A selection in your reader, preferably an essay

2. A chapter or section of a textbook

3. An article in a magazine

4. An editorial in a newspaper

5. A television or stage play

6. A movie

7. The main plots of a novel

8. The main points of a how-to article

9. The steps to follow in building something

10. The chronology of a trip or expedition

APPENDIX

A TYPICAL GRADE SHEET

A: The *A* theme shows originality of statement and observation. Its ideas are clear, logical, and even thought provoking. It contains all the positive qualities of good writing listed below:

    1. Careful construction and organization of sentences and paragraphs.

    2. Careful choice of effective words and phrases.

    3. Adequate development of idea, or inclusion of necessary details.

    4. Absence of mechanical errors.

B: The *B* theme is logically and adequately developed. Its ideas are developed clearly because it contains some of the positive qualities of good writing. It is comparatively free of errors in the use of English. Although indicating competence, the *B* paper lacks the originality of thought and style which characterizes the *A* theme.

C: The average theme will receive a grade of *C*. It is fairly well organized and manages to convey its purpose to the reader. It avoids serious errors in the use of English. It may, in fact, have few corrections marked on it; but it lacks the vigor of thought and expression which would entitle it to a better grade.

D: The grade of *D* indicates below average achievement in expression and effectiveness. Most *D* themes contain serious errors in the use of English and fail to convey adequately the purpose of the paper. With more careful proofreading and better development, many *D* themes could be worth at least a *C* rating.

F: A grade of *F* indicates the failure to avoid serious errors in spelling, grammar, punctuation, and sentence structure. No matter how excellent the content of the paper may be, the grade of *F* will be assigned if too many gross errors appear.

HOW TO BEGIN A THEME

A good first paragraph seems very difficult. A good first sentence seems almost beyond an inexperienced writer's creative powers. What years of time are wasted by high school and college students just trying to get started! But just as there are always ways of planning a paper, there are also ways of planning an effective beginning.

Remember that the purpose of an introductory paragraph is to catch the reader's attention in any one of a variety of ways. While doing so, the writer must try to give a kind of capsule outline of what he is going to do in his theme. This outline will depend entirely upon what type of theme he is writing: summary, inductive, flashback, etc. For example, he may use pictorial details, chronological incidents, illustrative instances, a definition, an enumeration, multiple reasons, or state a comparison between two items. The beginning writer should concentrate on using tried-and-true methods, such as those enumerated below. When he feels more comfortable about his writing, he can strive for more original approaches. In each of the discussions of types of themes in this book, re-read the SUGGESTIONS and ANALYSIS sections for hints about how to go about getting started. Here are a few possible ways of beginning an expository theme:

1. By asking a question or a series of questions and then stating that you intend to provide answers.

2. By a pertinent quotation from a book of quotations, a teacher, an authority, etc.

3. By stating your topic. See DEDUCTIVE form.

4. By using narration—a few lines of dialogue which are pertinent. See FLASHBACK form.

5. By beginning at the beginning of a CHRONOLOGICAL development.

6. By being different. That is, using startling words, expressions, a little-known item of information or by stating that a popular opinion is wrong, and the like. Do not use this approach unless you are sure of yourself.

7. By restating your title (and/or thesis sentence). Since your title and thesis sentence are not part of the theme, this device is frequently necessary.

8. By stating that you or somebody else once had an experience that the reader will find interesting, informative, etc.

9. By selecting a different, novel, interesting topic to write about and by telling the reader that he may find it interesting. Note that the suggested topics which follow each selection of themes are in general not topics of this sort.

10. By beginning with a dependent clause: When I was a boy ... If you should happen to travel through ... Since many people do not know that ... Because my teachers are ... Although most people have not seen ...

HOW TO CONCLUDE A THEME

Like the beginning, the ending is an important part of a theme. Because it contains the last words that the reader sees, it should be emphatic and effective, making a final impression upon the reader.

There is one important principle about ending themes that inexperienced writers tend to forget: When you have said all you intend to say, stop! A rambling and wordy ending will destroy the effect of what has been said. A short theme usually requires no formal conclusion; a summarizing or rounding-off sentence is usually sufficient. Your theme should leave an impression of completeness, of having rounded out a discussion and reached a goal. Avoid closing with a statement that concerns only a minor detail. Bring the reader to some phase of the main thought of your theme or leave him with a thought that is a new contribution to the subject.

Effective endings are often illustrated in the closing sentence or sentences of magazine articles. Study these for helpful hints. In addition, reread the sample themes and the SUGGESTIONS and ANALYSIS sections of this book where the conclusions of themes are suggested or discussed in principle. Also study the basic techniques for ending themes enumerated below:

1. It may end with a question: "Are we going to let this situation continue?"

2. It may end with a quotation pertaining to your topic.

3. It may repeat your opening topic. See CLASSIC form.

4. It may be the generalization to which your points have led. See INDUCTIVE form.

5. It may be a restatement of your choice of one thing over another. See ARGUMENT form.

6. It may be that you make a choice of one among many. See COMPARE AND CONTRAST form.

7. It may be a simple statement that you have presented the facts, suggesting that the reader make up his own mind. See IMPLIED form.

8. It may criticize one or the other (or both) of the sides you have presented. You could also state that the correct answer is somewhere in between.

9. It may suggest or prophesy that, henceforth, things will be different.

10. It may suggest other essays, articles, books, or the like, which the reader could read to further his knowledge of the subject you have discussed.

11. It may be a personal opinion, additional information, a vow, a promise, a warning, or a declaration of intent.

12. It may be a promise to the reader that if the instructions, etc., are followed, success will be his. See HOW-TO form.

DO NOT CONCLUDE:

1. With an apology to the reader for your ignorance, for lack of time, lack of interest, or the like.

2. By introducing another topic or detail.

3. With trite sayings like "Tired, but happy..." and the like.

4. By leaving the reader in doubt as to your meaning. See IMPLIED form.

5. With words, phrases, or sentences like "The End," "Finish," "I can't think of anything else."

DEFINITIONS

GENERALITIES: Expressions which are vague, all-inclusive, too abstract, too general, or those which are based on insufficient proof. Handbooks devote many pages to this error. See sections labeled "Exactness," "Wordiness," "Unity," "Logical Thinking," "Emphasis," "Diction," and the like. Avoid expressions like these: "Everyone knows," "It is obvious that," "It is always," and the like. See QUALIFIERS, below.

PARAGRAPH: A group of sentences controlled by a topic sentence. The usual practice in themes is to have each paragraph discuss one topic or topics that are closely related. Most of the paragraphs of the sample themes in this book are illustrative of this method of construction.

QUALIFIERS: Many freshmen have trouble with over-generalizing, using statements that are too broad (see GENERALITIES, above). Accordingly, a safe and more nearly correct way to write is to use qualifying words and expressions; examples are given in the following list:

apparently	in many instances
appears	in many cases
frequently	it seems to me
if	it is becoming
maybe	it is often the case
may	one of the ways
might	a random selection
often	for the purposes of discussion
occasionally	to my way of thinking
possibly, possible	some of us
probably, probable	in my limited experience
perhaps	if figures don't lie

Another way to qualify writing is to use the comparative degree of adjectives: *better* rather than *best*, *smoother* rather than *smoothest*, *worse* rather than *worst*, *more nearly perfect* rather than *most nearly perfect*, and so on.

THESIS: Usually one sentence placed below the title and apart from the body of the theme. It concentrates on an exact statement of what the theme is to prove, to explain, to argue, to describe, and so on. Like the title, the thesis sentence is not part of the theme; therefore you cannot use it as your first sentence, nor can you refer to it by using a pronoun. Note that many themes state the thesis in the first paragraph rather than setting it off by itself, which is preferable.

TOPIC SENTENCE: One sentence which tells or summarizes what a paragraph is discussing. The usual theme will discuss about three or four parts of a thesis (see above). Therefore, the usual theme will develop three or four main paragraphs.

TRANSITION: A word, phrase, sentence, or paragraph which tells the reader that you are going to another point, topic, or item. See the list of words and phrases in Number 11 of the PROOFREADING CHART. All handbooks have a section devoted to transitions. Where appropriate, such as in a HOW-TO theme, be particularly sure that each of your paragraphs which develop the topic sentences of your thesis begins in a similar matter: The first point, The second point, and the like. This technique lends an overall unity to your discussion; it also provides an easy method of transition from one paragraph to the next.

PROOFREADING CHART

1. Title: Do not underline or put in quotations. Do not place a period at the end of the title. However, do use a question mark or an exclamation point if warranted. Capitalize the first word of the title and all other words *except* articles, prepositions, and conjunctions. See the themes presented in this book.

2. Thesis: See DEFINITIONS.

3. Format: Neatness, margins, and so on. Follow your teacher's instructions or consult one of the handbooks listed in the BIBLIOGRAPHY.

4. Check for all errors made on previous themes.

5. Check all spelling.

6. Do all subjects and verbs agree?

7. Do all pronouns refer exactly to the antecedents?

8. Are all sentences complete?

9. Do you have any comma splices? See 11, below.

10. Check all pronouns. Especially check for right case. Especially check these singular pronouns: each, every, everyone, either, neither, another, anybody, anything, someone, somebody, something, one, everything, nobody, nothing. Also check these words: its, whose, theirs, his, hers, yours, ours. Remember that "it's" means "it is," "who's" means "who is," and "there's" means "there is."

11. If the following words and phrases link two independent sentences, use either a period or a semicolon before them: afterward, accordingly, also, anyhow, besides, consequently, furthermore, hence, however, indeed, instead, later, likewise, meanwhile, moreover, nevertheless, so, still, then, therefore, thereupon, thus, yet. Also these: at length, after all, at the same time, as a result, for instance, for example, in any event, in fact, in other words, in addition, in brief, in sum, on the contrary, on the other hand, that is.

12. Use either a singular or a plural verb with the following words, depending upon the subject which follows: here, there, where, who, why, what, when, how, none, all, more, most, some.

13. Transitions. See DEFINITIONS and 11, above.

14. All punctuation. Especially check for comma splices, conjunctive adverbs (see 11, above), and apostrophes.

15. Check pairs for correct spelling. Particularly dangerous are the following: accept-except, affect-effect, to-too, here-hear, there-their, it's-its, who's-whose, principle-principal, quit-quiet-quite, site-sight-cite, and words like lose-loose, chose-choose.

BIBLIOGRAPHY

The following handbooks and rhetorics are currently in use in colleges and universities and have discussions pertaining to theme writing. Check the table of contents in each text for the appropriate sections.

Baker, Sheridan. *The Practical Stylist*. 7th ed. New York: Harper and Row, 1990.

Barnet, Sylvan, and Marcia Stubbs. *Practical Guide to Writing*. 6th ed. Glenview, IL: Scott, Foresman, 1990.

Bauman, M. Garrett. *Ideas and Details: A Guide to College Writing*. Fort Worth, TX: Harcourt Brace Jovanovich, 1992.

Brooks, Cleanth, and Robert Penn Warren. *Modern Rhetoric*. 4th ed. New York: Harcourt Brace Jovanovich, 1979.

Campbell, Dianna. *Easy Writer: A Process and Sentence-Combining Approach to College Writing*. 3rd ed. New York: Harper Collins College Publishers, 1993.

Donald, Robert B., and others. *Writing Clear Paragraphs*. 4th ed. Englewood Cliffs, NJ: Prentice Hall, 1991.

Hodges, John C., and others. *Harbrace College Handbook*. 11th ed. Fort Worth, TX: Harcourt Brace Jovanovich, 1990.

Leggett, Glen, and others. *Prentice-Hall Handbook for Writers*. 11th ed. Englewood Cliffs, NJ: Prentice Hall, 1990.

Madden, Janet, and Sara M. Blake. *Crosscurrents: Themes for Developing Writers*. Fort Worth, TX: Harcourt Brace Jovanovich, 1992.

Morris, Alton C., and others. *College English*. 8th ed. New York: Harcourt Brace Jovanovich, 1983.

Nadell, Judith, and others. *The Macmillan Writer*. New York: Macmillan, 1991.

Rorabacher, Louise E. *Assignments in Exposition*. 9th ed. New York: Harper & Row, 1988.

Teitelbaum, Harry. *How To Write Book Reports*. New York: Arco Publishing, Simon & Schuster, 1989.

_____. *How To Write a Thesis*. 3rd ed. New York: Arco Publishing, Simon & Schuster, 1994.

Trimmer, Joseph F., and James M. McCrimmon. *Writing with a Purpose*. 10th ed. Boston: Houghton Mifflin, 1991.

Watkins, Floyd C., and others. *Practical English Handbook*. 9th ed. Boston: Houghton Mifflin, 1991.

Winkler, Anthony, and Jo Ray McCuen. *Rhetoric Made Plain*. 5th ed. New York: Harcourt Brace Jovanovich, 1988.

ACHEBE - Things Fall Apart
AESCHYLUS - The Plays
ARISTOTLE - The Philosophy
AUSTEN - Emma/Mansfield Park
AUSTEN - Pride and Prejudice
BECKETT - Waiting for Godot
Beowulf
BRADBURY- The Martian Chronicles
BRONTE - Jane Eyre
BRONTE - Wuthering Heights
BUCK - The Good Earth
CAMUS - The Stranger
CERVANTES - Don Quixote
CHAUCER - Canterbury Tales
CHEKHOV - The Plays
CHOPIN - The Awakening
CONRAD - Heart of Darkness/Secret Sharer
CONRAD - Lord Jim
CRANE - Red Badge of Courage
DANTE - The Divine Comedy
DE BEAUVOIR- The Second Sex
DESCARTES - The Philosophy
DICKENS - David Copperfield
DICKENS - Great Expectations
DICKENS - Hard Times
DICKENS - Oliver Twist
DICKENS - A Tale of Two Cities
DINESEN - Out of Africa
DOCTOROW- Ragtime
DONNE - The Poetry & The Metaphysical
Poets
DOSTOYEVSKY - Brothers Karamazov
ELIOT - Silas Marner
ELIOT - Murder in the Cathedral & Poems
ELLISON - Invisible Man
EURIPIDES - The Plays
FAULKNER - As I Lay Dying
FAULKNER - Light in August
FAULKNER - The Sound and the Fury
FIELDING - Joseph Andrews
FIELDING - Tom Jones
FITZGERALD - The Great Gatsby
FITZGERALD - Tender is the Night
FLAUBERT - Madame Bovary/Three Tales
FROST - The Poetry
GARCÍA-MÁRQUEZ - One Hundred Years
of Solitude
GOETHE - Faust

GOLDING - Lord of the Flies
Greek and Roman Classics
GREENE - The Power and the Glory
HAMMETT - The Maltese Falcon/Thin Man
HARDY - The Mayor of Casterbridge
HARDY - The Return of the Native
HARDY - Tess of the D'Urbervilles
HAWTHORNE - House of the Seven Gables/
Marble Faun
HAWTHORNE - The Scarlet Letter
HELLER - Catch-22
HEMINGWAY- A Farewell to Arms
HEMINGWAY - For Whom the Bell Tolls
HEMINGWAY - Major Works
HEMINGWAY - The Old Man and the Sea
HEMINGWAY - The Sun Also Rises
HOMER - The Iliad
HOMER - The Odyssey
HUXLEY - Major Works
IBSEN - The Plays
JAMES - The Turn of the Screw
JOYCE - A Portrait of the Artist as a Young
Man
KAFKA - The Trial
KEATS - The Poetry
KNOWLES - A Separate Peace
LAWRENCE - Sons and Lovers
LEE - To Kill A Mockingbird
LEGUIN - The Left Hand of Darkness
LEWIS - Babbitt
LOCKE & HOBBES - The Philosophies
MACHIAVELLI - The Prince/The Discourses
MARLOWE - Dr. Faustus
MELVILLE - Billy Budd
MELVILLE - Moby Dick
MILLER - The Crucible/A View from the
Bridge
MILLER - Death of a Salesman
MILTON - Paradise Lost
MORRISON - Beloved
Mythology
NIETZSCHE - The Philosophy
O'NEILL - The Plays
ORWELL - Animal Farm
ORWELL - 1984
PATON - Cry the Beloved Country
PLATO - The Republic and Selected
Dialogues

POE - Tales and Poetry
REMARQUE - All Quiet on the Western
Front
SALINGER - Catcher in the Rye
SARTRE - No Exit/The Flies
SCOTT - Ivanhoe
SHAKESPEARE - Antony and Cleopatra
SHAKESPEARE - As You Like It
SHAKESPEARE - Hamlet 2E
SHAKESPEARE - Henry IV, Part 1
SHAKESPEARE - Henry IV, Part 2
SHAKESPEARE - Julius Caesar
SHAKESPEARE - King Lear
SHAKESPEARE - Macbeth
SHAKESPEARE - The Merchant of Venice
SHAKESPEARE - A Midsummer Night's
Dream
SHAKESPEARE - Othello
SHAKESPEARE - Richard II
SHAKESPEARE - Richard III
SHAKESPEARE - Romeo and Juliet
SHAKESPEARE - Selected Comedies
SHAKESPEARE - The Taming of the Shrew
SHAKESPEARE - The Tempest
SHAKESPEARE - A Winter's Tale
SHAKESPEARE - Twelfth Night
SOPHOCLES - The Plays
SPENSER - The Faerie Queene
STEINBECK - The Grapes of Wrath
STEINBECK - Major Works
STEINBECK - Of Mice and Men
STEINBECK - The Pearl/Red Pony
SWIFT - Gulliver's Travels
THACKERAY - Vanity Fair/Henry Esmond
THOREAU - Walden
TOLSTOY - War and Peace
TWAIN - Huckleberry Finn
TWAIN - Tom Sawyer
VIRGIL - The Aeneid
VOLTAIRE - Candide/The Philosophies
WALKER - The Color Purple
WHARTON - Ethan Frome
WILDE - The Plays
WILDER - Our Town/Bridge of San Luis Rey
WILLIAMS - The Glass Menagerie
WILLIAMS - A Streetcar Named Desire
WOOLF - Mrs. Dalloway/To the Lighthouse
WRIGHT - Native Son

"HOW TO" GUIDES

How to Interpret Poetry

How to Read and Write About Fiction

How to Write Book Reports

How to Write Poetry

How to Write Research Papers

How To Write Short Stories

How to Write Themes and Essays

How to Write a Thesis

AVAILABLE AT BOOKSTORES EVERYWHERE

MACMILLAN • USA

Other fine references from

Webster's
NewWorld®

Webster's New World™ Encyclopedia

Webster's New World™ Encyclopedia
Pocket Edition

Webster's New World Dictionary®
Third College Edition

Webster's New World™ Thesaurus
New Revised Edition

Webster's New World™
Compact Dictionary
of American English

Webster's New World™
Pocket Dictionary

Webster's New World™
Power Vocabulary

Webster's New World™
Speller/Divider

Webster's New World™
Misspeller's Dictionary

Webster's New World™
Compact School and Office Dictionary

AVAILABLE AT BOOKSTORES EVERYWHERE

MACMILLAN • USA

ℓ_I